ROOTED,
NOT
RUSHED

ROOTED, NOT RUSHED

Healing, Reclaiming, and Rising in a World That Told You to Shrink

Mairin Moore Cane

Published by Game Changer Publishing

Paperback ISBN: 978-1-968250-75-1

Hardcover ISBN: 978-1-968250-76-8

Digital ISBN: 978-1-968250-77-5

GC GAME CHANGER
PUBLISHING
www.GameChangerPublishing.com

Advance Praise

"Joining the SOS Sisterhood of Success, founded by the remarkable Mairin Cane, has been one of the most transformative experiences of my life—both professionally and personally. I came seeking support in business, and what I found was an unshakable circle of women who hold space, speak truth, and rise together.

Mairin has created more than a mastermind group—she's cultivated a sacred ecosystem of soul-led women committed to growth, impact, and deep inner work. The level of safety, connection, and brilliance in this space is unlike anything I've experienced. It's not just about strategy—it's about sovereignty. About healing. About remembering who we really are underneath the armor, the hustle, the roles we play.

Through this sisterhood, I've expanded in ways I didn't even know I was ready for. I've had breakthroughs that no business course or coaching container ever offered. I've been challenged to grow, to lead, to be seen—fully and unapologetically.

Mairin's gift is alchemy. She holds the space with fierce grace and unwavering presence. Her leadership is intuitive, potent, and deeply nourishing. If you are looking for a container that honors both your wild and your wisdom, your ambition and your authenticity—this is it.

SOS isn't just a mastermind. It's a movement. It's remembering. And it's a sisterhood I didn't know I needed until I was inside it."

—MM

"When I first learned about Mairin and saw the powerhouse she was in the community, I knew right away that I wanted the opportunity to work with her. My first meeting with her, at a small coffee shop and without even knowing her, inspired me to pivot in my small business, add more value to my members, and grow as a business owner.

Recently, as a member of the Sisterhood, I've been blessed to experience Mairin on a much deeper level. She is not only the real deal but also meets every situation with such empowerment that it makes me believe in the greatness I truly have within myself. The confidence I've gained through her mentorship has been absolutely priceless.

For the first time, I've been able to set aside the identity tied to the businesses I built and discover who I am as an individual. Mairin has consistently supported my dreams while also providing the direction, guidance, and tangible next steps I needed to move to the next level. Without a doubt, she is top-notch. I am so grateful for her leadership."

—JL

"I signed up with Mairin because I was looking to up-level my business contacts and connections, go deeper with my business, and develop a new business model.

At the first meeting, with introductions, came quite a bit of personal story and conversation, which left my business brain spinning a little bit. For the second meeting, I thought all the "personal" stuff was out of the way so that we could focus on getting down to business. What I experienced was more discussion about our personal journeys through difficult times. It was raw, deep, and—at first— still confusing to my business brain.

What I discovered through this is that having a place where we can find support for our personal, messy journeys allows each member to go out into the business world and get things done. Each member of her group feels seen and heard, which leaves them motivated to tackle the business they need to.

I learned through her group that I had it backwards: to find business success, you need to start inward so you can see the success outward. By being part of this group, I've gained friendships and business success I would not have had otherwise. Thank you!"

—RL

"Being part of Mairin's Sisterhood of Success has been one of the most meaningful experiences of my author journey. From the very beginning, Mairin has walked alongside me with unwavering encouragement, wisdom, and genuine support.

Mairin's leadership is extraordinary. Her attention to detail and her heart for people make every interaction feel intentional and personal. She has a beautiful gift for making each woman feel seen, valued, and empowered. She doesn't just cheer from the sidelines—she gets in the trenches with you. Whether it's one-on-one check-ins to help us stay focused on our goals or the thoughtful ways she encourages growth, Mairin is the real deal.

I'm beyond grateful for the sisterhood, the structure, and the soul-deep support she provides. It has truly elevated my journey as an author and inspired me to keep moving forward with confidence and clarity."

—MB

For The Ones Still Becoming

For the ones who've fought silently,
healed slowly, and kept showing up:
May you feel seen in these pages
and reminded of your strength.

Read This First

Thank you for choosing to spend time with these words.

Your presence here matters to me.
Let's keep in touch as you walk your rooted and rising path.

Scan the QR Code Here:

SCAN ME

ROOTED,
NOT
RUSHED

Healing, Reclaiming, and Rising
In A World That Told You to Shrink

MAIRIN MOORE CANE

Foreword

There are seasons in life when the ground beneath us shifts—sometimes without warning.

A relationship changes. A dream ends. A door we thought would always be open quietly closes. In those moments, it's tempting to grasp for the fastest fix, to push harder, to rush our way back to "normal."

But rushing rarely brings peace. It only fuels exhaustion.

That's why *Rooted, Not Rushed* is such a gift. In these pages, Mairin Moore Cane offers an invitation to do something countercultural—something brave: slow down, plant your feet, and find your strength not in frantic motion, but in steady, grounded growth.

I've had the privilege of working alongside Mairin and seeing firsthand the incredible work she's doing through her gatherings, coaching, and retreats. She creates spaces where women feel seen, heard, and supported—spaces that inspire transformation from the inside out. I felt an immediate connection with her because, although our journeys are different, our hearts beat for the same mission: to help women rise with resilience and purpose. We need more women in the world who lift each other up, and that is exactly what Mairin does—every single day.

Foreword

She doesn't write from a distant mountaintop. She writes from the messy middle—where the air is thick with uncertainty, where grief and transition meet resilience and hope. With unflinching honesty, Mairin shares her own stories of loss, rebuilding, and transformation, making you feel less alone in your own.

But this is more than encouragement—it's a guidebook. Mairin weaves together personal storytelling, clear takeaways, and practical exercises that help you:

- Rest without guilt and listen for what your soul truly needs.
- Reframe setbacks into stepping stones.
- Anchor yourself in values that bring clarity in uncertainty.
- Build small, sustainable rhythms that restore your energy and hope.

This isn't a book you'll read once and tuck away. It's one you'll return to whenever life feels unsteady—a steady hand to hold in the pause before the rise.

So take a deep breath. Let these pages remind you: you don't have to rush to rise. You can root yourself deeply, live with intention, and step forward with courage—no matter what season you're in.

—*Amberly Lago*
USA Today Bestselling Author, TEDx Speaker,
Coach, Top 1% Podcast Host

Contents

Letter to the Reader

Dear You:

There will come a day when you'll forget how far you've come.

When you'll look at your reflection and only see the pieces that are still healing.

When the world feels too loud again.

When you'll wonder if you've actually made any progress at all.

So before we begin, let me say this:

You are not behind.

You are not failing because you feel tired.

You are not weak because you need rest.

You are not broken because you're still becoming.

You are living a life that most people don't see—the invisible work of waking up and choosing to keep going.

You are learning to tell the truth without apologizing.

You are learning to speak your needs, even if your voice still shakes.

You are learning to take up space in your own story.

And you've already done so much more than survive.

You're still here.

You're still trying.

You're still listening to your own voice, and that matters.

So, if you ever doubt it again, come back to this page.

Come back to the part of you that knew you deserved more.

Come back to the you who decided this story was worth telling.

Come back to the one who said, "This is where I begin again."

This book wasn't written just for you to read.

It was written for you to *live with*.

You'll notice space to reflect throughout these pages—pause moments, journal prompts, and a complete companion workbook at the back. These aren't just extras. They're invitations. To slow down. To see yourself more clearly. To connect with the you who's still unfolding.

Don't worry about doing it perfectly.

Just meet yourself honestly.

And let these pages rise up to meet you, wherever you are.

With you,
Mairin Moore Cane

Preface
A Moment of Collapse and Awakening

I've lived through more ups and downs than most would believe if I told them all at once.

From early childhood trauma to the relentless pressure of running a business across thirty-four states, I was constantly navigating high stress, often in silence.

I was a high performer—I always had been. I found my worth in my productivity, my purpose in my output. I stayed "on" for everyone, pouring everything I had into being needed, useful, and dependable.

Control wasn't just a preference—it was how I survived.

But in 2020, everything changed.

Just before the world shut down, I found myself on a trip, face-to-face with a Category 3 tornado just blocks away. It was a terrifying, surreal moment, but I didn't know then that it was just the beginning.

When I returned home, the world entered lockdown—and so did I. My body, worn down from years of chronic stress, simply stopped working.

It didn't know how to process. It didn't know how to keep going. I went from making high-level decisions and leading teams across the country to being bedridden, trapped in a body that no longer responded to me.

There was no fixing it, no performing my way out, no plan, no schedule, no drive that could reverse what was happening.

And that's when I realized how much of my identity had been wrapped in the "doing," the giving, and the proving.

Without it, I felt exposed, unsafe, unworthy.

I had built a life staying off radars that felt unknown or unsafe to me— hustling in the background, showing up for others, people-pleasing to avoid pain, rejection, or being forgotten.

But when I could no longer do it, I had to face who I was beneath it all.

The stillness, though brutal, became my reckoning. It was there—in the quiet, in the undoing—that healing began for me.

When I stopped resisting and let life unfold, I learned to accept the limits of what I could shape. That acceptance became the starting point for my recovery and eventually, for my rebirth.

Chapter 1
What I Thought Was Strength

"She stood in the storm, and when the wind did not
blow her way, she adjusted her sails."
—Elizabeth Edwards

Long before my body gave out, I learned to survive.

That survival looked a lot like strength on the outside—independence, drive, responsibility, and the ability to keep going no matter what. People called me "strong," and I believed them. I wore that word like armor.

But what most people didn't see was that my strength was born out of necessity, not choice.

It came from childhood experiences that taught me early on that safety was not guaranteed, love had to be earned, and control was a means of protecting myself.

Somewhere along the way, I internalized a dangerous equation: *My value = What I can do for others.* Not because I wasn't truly intending to help, support, or give, but there was an added benefit for me that kept me safe and sheltered with what I felt was a protection.

That belief system became the blueprint for how I lived. I became a master at holding everything together for everyone. I found comfort in systems, purpose in pressure, and validation in productivity.

The higher I climbed, the more invisible the cracks became.

Looking back, I can see how early trauma and chronic stress wove themselves into every corner of my life. I didn't know it at the time, but I was running on survival mode for years.

And the world rewarded me for it.

That's the tricky thing: When you're excellent at functioning in dysfunction, no one questions you. You become reliable, admirable, even enviable. But deep down, there's a cost.

The cost for me was disconnection from my body, from my needs, from my truth.

I was constantly "on," but rarely present. I built a life that appeared successful, but I was slowly fading from within.

I thought I was thriving. I was actually bracing.

I was waiting for the next thing and holding my breath in between the chaos.

And then, everything caught up with me.

But before I tell you about the collapse, I need to tell you about the foundations because you don't truly understand the power of rebuilding until you understand what the storm swept away.

I didn't realize it back then, but the way I showed up in the world was shaped by experiences for which I had no language, only reactions.

As a child, I learned how to read a room before I even knew how to read words. I could sense tension. I could feel when something was off. And like so many kids who've been through trauma, I did what I needed to do to feel safe: I adapted.

I became helpful and quiet when needed to be, smiling even when it hurt. I didn't know I was building a survival strategy; I thought I was doing what was expected of me.

I didn't just want to be loved; I wanted to be predictable. The more chaos there was around me, the more I tried to control what was within me.

If I could be perfect, maybe no one would yell.

If I could be quiet, maybe I wouldn't get hurt.

If I could be helpful, maybe they'd want me around.

Those small compromises of self didn't feel like choices at the time. They felt like survival.

I learned to read a room before I ever learned to read a book. I studied expressions. I listened for footsteps. I memorized moods. And I bent myself to fit them—until I didn't even know what shape I was anymore.

Over time, those coping mechanisms grew into traits the world applauds: responsibility, independence, and strength.

While those traits helped me survive, they also taught me to bypass my own needs, disconnect from my emotions, and believe that love and safety were things I had to earn.

I wasn't taught how to rest; I was taught how to hustle. I wasn't taught how to feel; I was taught how to fix.

And so I became a fixer, a doer, and a person people could count on, even when I couldn't count on myself.

That version of me carried me far. It got me through school, into leadership roles, and eventually into building something bigger from the ground up. I created success out of sheer grit. And on the surface, it looked like I had it all figured out.

But underneath it, I was still that little girl, quietly scanning for safety. Quietly wondering if I was enough.

My mom, a single parent navigating her own wounds at the time of my early childhood, did everything she could to hold things together. She loved me deeply, and I know that now more than ever. But love doesn't erase struggle. And sometimes, as a child, I recall having to step into roles that felt bigger than myself—trying to help, trying to steady, trying to be "enough" to make it all okay.

With my dad, the relationship was vastly different. Visits were often over-shadowed by conflict between my parents, so much so that I remember more tension than togetherness when I was with them. I can still recall moments that felt like they shaped my entire understanding of safety and complex relationships: being told to manage and call my dad regarding late child support payments, or witnessing physical moments that no child should ever have to see.

And while I saw spankings and punishments to my two sisters while at my dad's, I was never one to receive them myself. Surprisingly, while no one likes punishment, the lack of attention felt more like neglect than anything else.

But it kept me safe.

I felt that if I was quiet and didn't upset anyone, I would avoid being on the radar. Later, that quiet became even more imperative for my safety in life, as it protected my body in ways that, with others, I still cannot and do not wish to speak of.

I don't share these things to blame my life and my situations or to put a "label" on why things have become as they have, but to acknowledge the impact.

When children grow up in emotional chaos—even when love is present—they learn to perform for peace.

Maybe you've been there too. Maybe you learned how to read the room before you even understood your own emotions. Maybe, like me, you grew up trading parts of yourself for the comfort of others.

We don't always realize it at the time, but that kind of wiring follows us into our relationships, our work, and our sense of worth.

It doesn't make us weak. It means we adapted. We survived.

But eventually, if we want to live—not just survive—we have to go back and meet those parts of ourselves with compassion.

Because we're not here to earn love. We're here to receive it.

That's the quiet heartbreak of high performers. We are often praised for how much we can carry, when what we need is someone to say, "You don't have to carry it all alone." And after doing that for so long, I can honestly say I didn't know what to do or how to react when someone finally did.

I used to think strength was about keeping it all in. I thought silence was safer, and stillness made me noble.

But silence has a cost, and eventually, the debt came due.

I paid for it with my body:

With anxiety I couldn't explain.

With exhaustion that sleep couldn't touch.

With tears that came out of nowhere and a constant sense of not being "enough," no matter how hard I worked to prove I was.

It turns out that the strength we use to survive isn't always the same strength we need to heal. And the truth I had to face was this: You cannot grow into your fullest self while shrinking to stay safe.

My body did what my voice never dared to do.

It said: *Stop.*

It forced a pause I never would have chosen, and unraveled everything I had built around being needed, productive, and "strong."

That was the beginning of everything breaking. And, as I'd come to learn, the beginning of everything becoming.

Looking back, the signs didn't start with collapse. They had been whispering to me for years: soft, subtle clues that my life was out of rhythm with what I truly needed.

I was diagnosed with celiac disease nearly two decades ago, shortly after my son was born. I adjusted my lifestyle, learned how to navigate it, and stayed vigilant, careful with what I ate, what I touched, and how I lived. But even with all that effort, my body kept finding ways to remind me that something wasn't right.

By 2015, I began noticing patterns I couldn't ignore: Food wasn't staying in. Cross-contamination, no matter how cautious I was, seemed inevitable. I'd eat, and minutes later I'd be rushing to the bathroom—sometimes to vomit, sometimes doubled over in pain, often both. The joy I once felt around food was replaced by dread.

My digestive system had stopped behaving like it belonged to me.

My bowels became unpredictable and violent. Each day came with a weight I couldn't shake: Nausea that overwhelmed my world in a consistent and unrelenting way. The panic showed up in surges—sudden, sharp, and hard to predict. It felt like my body and my mind were unraveling at the same time. Every episode of nausea triggered panic attacks: sudden, uncontrollable surges of fear that left me shaking, breathless, and terrified that I wouldn't or couldn't continue any further.

By the time 2020 arrived, the gentle warnings had become alarm bells. I was losing weight quickly. Not because I wanted to or was doing something to invite it. By the height of the COVID-19 pandemic, I had dropped to 96 pounds. My blood pressure was so high it became dangerous, often soaring to 200/150.

In October 2020, it happened. I was rushed to the hospital: My blood pressure spiked so violently they feared a stroke or heart attack.

I stayed there for weeks.

The irony wasn't lost on me: I had spent a lifetime trying to stay in control of circumstances, emotions, outcomes. And now, the very things I had ignored—my capacity, my energy, my needs—I could no longer override.

After test after test, appointment after appointment, theory after theory, I was diagnosed with Gastroparesis, tachycardia, and an unknown form of dysautonomia, a dysfunction of the autonomic nervous system that, years later, still has no clear cause or tracking.

And then, when I thought my body had already surrendered everything it could, I got COVID.

The virus took what was already fragile and broke it wide open. I had high fevers of an average of 104 degrees every day for four months. Nausea became constant and unrelenting. My nervous system seemed to forget how to function entirely. When the active COVID left, it also left me wholly changed.

I have spent years now fighting to avoid feeding tubes, fighting a shutdown of parts of my body and overcompensations, and fighting to regain balance, and fighting to live—not just *exist*.

~

My sense of stability began to break down in ways most people never have to think about.

Simple functions, once automatic, became uncertain. And with each new limitation came a fresh wave of grief I had no time to process.

The malnutrition began to affect my mind: I struggled to find words. I'd trip over sentences. Thoughts slipped away before I could speak them. I felt like a ghost in my own life—here, but not fully present.

And with all of that came the silent companion that often follows long-term illness: depression. This wasn't just sadness, but a kind of profound, soul-level fatigue, the ache of being trapped in a body that no longer responded to the will of the spirit inside it.

But this is not a story of sickness. This is a story of becoming.

It's the story of what it means to be taken to your edge, whether by health, heartbreak, burnout, or grief, and to still choose to rebuild. It's about what it means to lose everything you thought made you "strong" and discover something deeper.

One moment from that season, late 2022, is forever imprinted in my memory:

It was my son's senior homecoming, the kind of milestone that should be marked with joy, celebration, and photos taken in the front yard of your home as the beautiful couple exchanges corsages and boutonnieres before their evening of fun. And I was in a hospital bed, IVs in my arm, praying I wouldn't miss it entirely.

But the hospital staff—generous, compassionate, and probably bending more rules than they were allowed—snuck him and his date in so I could be part of the moment.

They stood before me, so polished, so full of excitement and life. And there I was, in a hospital gown, sitting beside them in a wheelchair, smiling for a picture I never imagined would happen this way.

I still have that photo. My smile is soft, but full—layered with pride, pain, and an overwhelming sense of presence. I had made it to one of the most critical moments in his childhood, not in the way I'd expected it to turn out to be, but *I was there.*

That image lives in my heart not because it was perfect, but because it was *real.*

And that day reminded me of something I had nearly forgotten: that love doesn't need grand gestures. Presence—however messy, imperfect, or fragile—is everything.

And the truth is that moment was never just about one child.

I have multiple children, and they were, and are still, each my reason: my drive to stay alive, my reminder that this fight was bigger than me, my ultimate "why to get up" each day.

I wanted them to see what it looks like to keep showing up *even when it's hard.* To know that we don't give up just because life gets unbearable. We pause. We rest. We fight differently. But we *do not give up.*

And through all of it—every raw, unfiltered moment—stood my husband.

I've always been fiercely independent, the one who took care of everything. But in this season, I had to learn to lean and to trust deeply in a way I'd never known before. I had to trust he was caring for the home while I couldn't, that he was the ultimate parent when I wasn't able, and that he was providing as the leader of our family.

He became more than my partner; he became my safe place. My best friend, yes, but also the only person who truly saw the depth of my pain as it was unfolding, day by day, behind closed doors.

He cared for me when I couldn't care for myself.

He coaxed me to eat when I had no energy left to even try.

He fought my battles when I no longer had the strength.

He advocated when my voice was too shaky to be heard.

He carried the weight of my survival alongside me, and never once did he make me feel like a burden for it. His love, quiet and steady, became part of the reason I kept choosing to stay.

Even when I couldn't stand on my own, I was standing for something: my children, my future, my own becoming.

This isn't just a story of what I lost. It's a story of who I became while learning to live with the loss.

Maybe I didn't want to be here. Not all the time. There were quiet, hollow moments when I thought it might be easier just to give up. I couldn't recognize the person I had become.

They say that when you're diagnosed with a chronic illness, you don't just fight the disease; you grieve the version of yourself that could do all the things you can't anymore. I missed her.

The me who could move freely, who had energy, loved food, laughed louder, and made plans—the me who didn't have to calculate her strength before getting out of bed.

But she was gone.

And all I had left was this unfamiliar version of myself: fragile, fatigued, in fear, and flickering like a light that couldn't quite stay on.

I just knew if this was the version of me that would survive, I didn't want to survive this way—not in this fog, carrying this level of sorrow in my bones.

I realized something I never expected to: I didn't just need to give up control over what was happening to me, I needed to give up *feeling the way I did* about myself.

I needed to stop clinging to the idea that healing meant returning to who I used to be, and start letting in the possibility of becoming someone new, not because I wanted this, but because I wanted *more* than this.

I wanted more life, more peace, more purpose than pain.

And that meant learning how to stay even when life was spiraling out of control. I had to learn how to choose life, even when I didn't like what life looked like.

That was the beginning—not of joy or clarity, but of *surrender to a willingness for the unknown and relinquishing control.*

And sometimes, that's enough.

Illness wasn't the only place I had to learn resilience. Life gave me lessons long before my body ever began to break.

I've rebuilt myself from disappointments I never saw coming—from betrayals that taught me how to trust differently, financial setbacks, heartbreaks, losses, and those quiet nights when I couldn't recognize the reflection staring back at me.

I've had to learn what it means to lead while carrying grief, to keep showing up for others while secretly falling apart inside, and to parent with presence even when I felt painfully absent from myself.

There have been seasons where everything felt like it was happening all at once: career stress, family pressure, health flares, relational tension, and still, I kept going. I persevered not because I was fearless, but because I didn't know how to give up.

Resilience isn't something I discovered in crisis. It's something I had been practicing long before I had language for it.

I've spent my life navigating uncertainty.

Balancing the weight of being the strong one.

Making peace with the silence that sometimes follows survival.

And somewhere along the way, I realized something:

Resilience isn't loud. It doesn't always roar.

Sometimes, resilience is a whisper that says: *I'm still here.*

Sometimes, it's doing the hard thing even when no one is watching.

Sometimes, it's forgiving yourself for being human.

And sometimes, it's starting over.

The truth is, I didn't just survive. I rebuilt.

One of the most pivotal moments of learning resilience through rebuilding came in 2016—before hospitals and diagnoses would test me in other ways, even as the weight of stress was already taking root in my body—when someone we trusted, someone we had partnered with for years, got greedy. Unbeknownst to us, this person had been quietly planning a strategic departure from our business for nearly two years. They planned to take everything so that we no longer needed to share potential profits.

And then, one day, he simply left.

What was left was the empty violation of abandonment from someone who was supposed to be on a short list of those I trusted, one who was supposed to be one of my oldest and best friends at the time.

He wiped his computer and duplicated all our work to take for himself, recruited nearly ninety percent of our team, and walked out to start a competing company.

We didn't know what was happening until it was almost too late.

In that moment, we could've folded. But instead, we did what we always did: We figured it out. While I stayed behind and rebuilt the business from the ground up, my husband took a job elsewhere to ensure our financial stability. It was never about stepping away but about stepping up in the way we needed at the time. We did what we had to do to survive.

And in that season, something shifted in me. I didn't just rebuild the business; I began building myself.

I restructured. I reimagined. I led.

Quietly. Relentlessly. Without applause.

In the years that followed that 2016 reckoning and rebuild, something more was created—not just within our original company but beyond it.

I founded new businesses of my own.

I stepped onto stages I once felt too small for.

I began consulting with major companies and their executives—Microsoft, Nike, VRBO, Amazon—bringing the kind of insight only someone who's *actually lived it* can offer.

I started to speak, not just to others, but *for myself.*

And somewhere in the middle of all that, I did something that terrified me: I applied for an international women's competition, something I never would've dreamed of doing years before. I made it to the final round. Out of more than 30,000 women, I placed fourth in the final round—not because I was the loudest or most polished, but because I showed up fully, vulnerably, authentically, and unapologetically as *me.*

I didn't do it to win.

I did it to finally *see myself*, and to let others see me, too.

For so long, I had been defined by everything *around* me, my marriage, my work, my illness, my roles, but this was a moment where I stepped fully *into* myself.

And once you do, you can't go back to being invisible.

You start living from a place of knowing: not *I'm strong because I have to be,* but *I'm strong because I finally chose me.*

Looking back now, I can see how the woman I was—strong, determined, rebuilding after betrayal and loss—also laid the foundation for the woman I would become.

I didn't know then what was coming.

I didn't know how deeply I'd be tested.

But I knew how to rise. I had been doing it for years.

What changed wasn't my strength.

What changed was the *shape* of it.

I used to believe resilience looked like pushing through.

Now I know it also looks like *pulling back*.

Like resting. Releasing. Redefining what it means to lead, love, and live in a world that doesn't slow down, even when your life demands it.

Maybe you've felt this too. Maybe you've been the one holding it all together. Maybe no one saw how hard you were working—not just in your job, or your home, but inside your own head and heart.

Maybe you've quietly rebuilt parts of your life after someone walked away, after something fell apart, after your reflection stopped looking like someone you recognized.

If so, I want you to hear this clearly: **You've already survived things you never thought you could.**

That's not nothing. That's not "just life." That's resilience.

You might not feel brave.

You might still feel broken, tired, and uncertain.

But you're here. And that counts for something.

Maybe you're in a chapter where everything feels unclear.

Maybe you're just now waking up to the realization that something needs to change, but you're not sure what, or how.

This isn't a book about having all the answers. It's a book about asking different questions—not *How do I get back to who I used to be?* but, *Who am I becoming now?*

INSIGHTS TO CONSIDER:

Researchers have found that early life adversity—such as emotional neglect, unpredictability, or chronic stress—can significantly affect the development of the brain's stress response system. But here's the good news: Those same systems can be reshaped through reflection, relational support, and safe environments.[1]

Resilience isn't about avoiding hardship; it's about how we adapt and grow through it.

BEFORE YOU TURN THE PAGE...

This chapter was my story.

Now, I invite you to look at your own.

You don't have to relate to every detail to recognize the patterns: the striving, the silence, the strength you didn't even know you had.

As you prepare to step into the next chapter, take a few moments to pause. Let the noise settle. Let your own truth rise.

Here are a few questions to help you reflect on where *you* are right now:

PAUSE AND REFLECT:

This isn't the end of your story. It's just a new way to begin.

1. Where have I been strong without realizing it?

Think back to moments you endured, adjusted, or rose when things were falling apart. You don't need a spotlight to be a survivor.

2. What version of me have I been grieving, even quietly?

Sometimes we carry grief not for a person, but for a former self—a role we lost, a way we used to move in the world, a time when things felt easier.

3. What have I been taught resilience should look like, and is that still serving me?

Reflect on where "strength" may have become performance. What would softer strength look like for you now?

4. Have I given myself permission to rest without guilt? To ask for help without shame?

True resilience includes restoration. Where can you let yourself breathe?

5. What truth am I ready to say out loud, to myself or to someone else, for the first time?

Healing often begins when we give voice to the things we've been carrying in silence.

You're allowed to evolve.
You're allowed to soften.
You're allowed to begin again.
Resilience isn't a demand; it's a deep remembering of who you are underneath what the world has asked you to carry.

Chapter 2
The Becoming Begins

"And the day came when the risk to remain tight in a bud
was more painful than the risk it took to blossom."
—Anaïs Nin

Becoming isn't one big, brave decision. It's a thousand quiet ones. And for me, they didn't come after I got better—because I never fully did.

I didn't realize how much of my identity was tied to performance until everything I used to perform stopped working.

Success, for me, wasn't just about building a business. It was about creating a sense of self-worth through the recognition it brought. I was a high performer, a top producer, someone who thrived in structure, results, and doing what others said couldn't be done. I started at twenty-one years old, launching a business out of my two-bedroom apartment with no formal experience—just grit, goals, and prayer. I never finished school, and as the business quickly took off, I never looked back. Over the next several years, we expanded into thirty-four states. Through my twenties and thirties, I built a reputation as a top producer, always pushing for the next win.

My sense of safety came from how useful I could be, how hard I could push, and how much I could juggle without ever dropping the ball.

At least, that's what it looked like from the outside.

I found purpose in my productivity, validation in being needed, and fulfillment in constantly creating.

But when the world stopped in 2020—and my body followed—I couldn't outrun it anymore.

I had to sit in what I had been avoiding for years: the question of who I was without the "doing."

Before that moment, I didn't know how to slow down. I was always on the move, always striving, always planning the next goal, meeting, launch, or idea. My calendar was full, my title was polished, and my image was tightly managed. I knew how to show up for the world, but not always how to show up for myself.

I had spent two decades of my life building companies—mine and others —consulting with other businesses, and showing up in every room with a curated mix of strength and "spit shine." From the outside, I was accomplished and driven. Inside, I was exhausted. My pace was unsustainable, and deep down, I knew it. But I kept going.

Because slowing down felt like failure.

I had always been seen as the strong one, the responsible one, the go-getter. My reputation became a mask I didn't know how to remove. And as long as people kept clapping, I kept dancing.

When I got truly, unavoidably sick in 2020, it wasn't one diagnosis but a series of escalating symptoms I could no longer ignore: unrelenting nausea, weight loss, joint pain, fatigue, and dangerously high blood pressure.

By 2023, I had been hospitalized more than a handful of times, for weeks on end, and spent three years mostly bedridden. Doctors had theorized incorrect diagnosis after diagnosis, but after years of unrelenting tests and theories, after pushing to be heard and seen in a medical system that speaks and treats to symptoms only, with hard advocacy for myself for all their lack of knowledge how to root to the cause of my pain and my health concerns, I was finally diagnosed with gastroparesis. This chronic illness results in paralysis of the gastrointestinal system, caused by intermittent dysfunction of the autonomic nervous system. This period, which unfolded during the peak of COVID-19, marked a complete shift in my reality—an isolation of self with no cure in an already locked-down world. I felt like I had lost everything that made me "me." I couldn't work like I used to. I couldn't lead like I used to. I couldn't serve others the way I was used to doing.

And suddenly, I felt all alone in understanding life and who I was. I felt entirely invisible.

Everything I had built seemed to crumble. And in that crumbling, I was forced to ask the hardest question of all: *Who am I if I'm not performing?*

At first, I didn't like the answer.

I had built a life around proving. I had wrapped my worth in my work, and when the work was gone, I was terrified that the worth went with it.

But here's what I learned: Becoming isn't about what you do; it's about who you are when there's nothing left to prove.

And that's where my healing began—not with another accomplishment, but with permission to be seen as human.

I was still in the thick of illness when something began to shift. I realized that this was my life now; it wasn't tied to a finish line, a successful "win," and in not waiting for a cure or a perfect resolution. My days rose and fell with flare-ups that came and went, some lasting hours, others weeks and months. Some stole my words, others stole my balance.

But even without all the answers, I found change. I stopped saying yes when my body whispered no. I stopped trying to control every variable in hopes of staying ahead of the pain. I stopped prioritizing what others needed from me and started honoring what my body needed.

I knew what it felt like to ignore the signs, and I knew what came next if I didn't protect myself. And I wasn't willing to betray my body again just to keep someone else comfortable.

And then, in 2024—still very much living with illness, but more willing to tell the truth about it—came a moment I didn't expect, one that changed everything. I was invited to speak at a women's event in my community. An entire community of women gathered in one large ballroom, and for the first time, I told the real and raw truth—not the polished version that kept people comfortable, but the real story I was holding.

I spoke about my health, my body, and the silent unraveling behind the scenes.

And when I finished, I didn't linger. I didn't stay to take pictures, mingle, or explain myself.

I walked out, not out of rudeness, but out of release.

It felt like an exhale, like offering the whole of me to the world for the first time and saying, "Do what you will. This is who I am now."

I went home that night and slept for twenty-eight hours straight. If you've ever doubted the emotional weight of truth-telling, let me tell you: Healing has a toll.

But that sleep and that silence were peace—the kind that only comes when you finally stop pretending.

The woman I'm becoming doesn't ask for approval. She doesn't perform for belonging.

She doesn't carry stories that aren't hers. She tells the truth. And then she rests.

For so long, I thought my value came from the outcome. Now, I know my value is present in the effort. In the breath. In the being.

This wasn't the end of my story. It was the unlearning of everything I thought I had to be. So I could finally become who I already was.

And that subtle, sacred, and uncomfortable shift became the foundation for everything that came next.

INSIGHTS TO CONSIDER:

1. Performance as Self-Worth Isn't Rare—But It's Risky

Research shows that people who tie their self-worth to achievement (what psychologists call *contingent self-esteem*) experience significantly more stress, anxiety, and burnout. When your identity is built around performance, rest starts to feel like failure, and overwork becomes a form of self-validation.[1]

✧ Reflect: Are you building from your truth or performing to prove something?

2. Burnout Isn't Just Exhaustion—It's Identity Erosion

Burnout isn't about being "tired." It's emotional depletion that comes when your output no longer feels aligned with your inner self. Studies show that long-term burnout is associated with detachment from one's values, decreased self-compassion, and even symptoms of depression.[2]

✧ Reflect: If you weren't "productive," who would you still be?

3. Rebuilding Identity Means You're Growing—Not Starting Over

When you step out of performance mode and into alignment, it can feel like you're "losing" who you were. But neurologically, your brain is just adapting to a new narrative. Neuroplasticity (your brain's ability to rewire itself) means every aligned decision you make reinforces a more integrated identity.[3]

✧ Reflect: What are you becoming more of, not less, by letting go of who you used to be?

BEFORE YOU TURN THE PAGE...

This chapter was my story.

Now, I invite you to look at your own.

Maybe you've been living with something chronic—something unseen, misunderstood, or unspoken.

Or maybe you've been performing strength in a life that hasn't allowed you to feel safe being soft.

You don't need to wait for a breakdown to begin your becoming.

Sometimes, healing starts with honesty.

Take a moment. Let your truth rise.

PAUSE AND REFLECT:

You don't have to be healed to be whole.

1. Where have you tied your identity to your performance?
2. What parts of yourself have you neglected while striving to "keep it all together?"
3. If you couldn't measure your worth by productivity or praise, what would you measure it by?
4. When was the last time you told the truth and then rested in it?
5. Who are you without the "doing"?
6. What would it look like to show up for yourself the way you show up for others?
7. If nothing changed around you, what would it look like to change how you see yourself?
8. What are you becoming, not someday, but right now?

You are not the version of you that needs to prove.
You are the version of you that gets to be.
You don't need permission to slow down.
You need the courage to stay honest.

Chapter 3
Living on Purpose

*"Almost everything will work again if you
unplug it for a few minutes... including you."*
—Anne Lamott

When I started living like I had nothing to prove, everything changed.

My "no" got stronger. My rest got sacred. My peace became a priority, not just a passing wish.

For most of my life, I had been busy being reliable, available, and impressive. And when I finally stopped showing up in ways that cost me my health or my joy, I realized something I hadn't expected: People adjust.

The ones who love you? They learn how to meet you where you are. The ones who only loved what you gave them? They disappear. And as hard as that is, it's also a gift.

I used to think boundaries would make me feel guilty. But in reality, they made me feel free.

I wasn't pushing people away; I was pulling myself back into my own alignment, my values, and into a life where I didn't have to trade my well-being to be seen.

I don't live fast anymore. I live on purpose.

I don't say yes out of fear. I say yes from trust.

I don't measure my value by what I produce. I measure it by how I feel and who I'm becoming in the process.

I used to live like my body was optional, like it was just a tool to carry out everything I thought I had to prove. But whether it's your body, your mind, or your soul, eventually something calls out for your attention.

And when it does, you don't just start listening. You start honoring.

And honoring myself meant changing everything. It meant turning down opportunities that once fed my ego. It meant skipping events I would have once forced myself to attend just to avoid disappointing someone else. It meant building a life where I no longer needed to "push through" in order to be seen as committed, strong, or successful.

Over the past year, since sharing my story out loud, I've been learning to build a new kind of rhythm, one shaped by the lessons I've been gathering since I got sick in 2020. Boundaries don't come quickly. They're like falling and getting back up again, learning each time. That speaking moment didn't make me perfect at it, but it gave me permission to start truly protecting those boundaries, so I wouldn't keep falling the same way.

I started building a new kind of rhythm, one that respected the days my body couldn't do what it used to. One that didn't punish me for needing rest.

I began asking different questions before making decisions: Does this bring me peace? Will this cost me more than it gives? Am I saying yes out of love or fear?

These questions changed the way I spoke, worked, and showed up in relationships.

And for the first time, I realized: Boundaries aren't just limits. They're invitations to live with clarity and without depletion. They're invitations to stay well, not just alive.

There are still days when I wake up with less capacity than I hoped for, when even the basics feel like mountains. But I no longer sacrifice myself just to keep everyone else comfortable.

That version of me is gone, and I don't miss her.

Some of the hardest boundaries I had to set were with people I'd known the longest: old friends and people who had loved the earlier version of me, the one who over-gave, overworked, and over-accommodated.

Instead of growing with me, they kept reminding me of who I used to be. And every time they did, it felt like I was being pulled away from healing, growth, and peace.

Eventually, I had to make a choice. And as painful as it was, I let some of them go, not in bitterness, but in liberation. Healing requires space, and some people just aren't meant to walk with you into the next chapter.

Another boundary that changed everything? Time.

I no longer allow others to take mine without care. Because life shifts in unexpected ways, I never know when my energy will crash or my capacity will change. I've learned to protect the hours I do feel well, because they're sacred. They're fuel. They're not guaranteed.

So I ask different questions now: Is this worth the energy it will cost me? Does this align with what I value, or just what I feel obligated to do?

I've redefined what success looks like in my days. It's no longer about how much I get done.

It's about how I feel while doing it.

During that season of profound depletion, I didn't have the luxury of overextending. I wasn't "busy." I wasn't curating a brand or chasing goals. I was simply responding to what my body allowed me to do each day. In that stillness, the truth began to surface.

So many of the habits I thought were just "who I am" were just who I'd been taught to be: performative, productive, people-pleasing.

When all of that fell away, I had to ask: *What do I actually value now?*

So I rebuilt my days, slowly. I began adding back only what served me. I reshaped my schedule with space for rest, nutrition, slowness, and joy. I let go of anything that didn't align with the life I wanted to live, or the version of me I was becoming. At first, it was very calculatory in terms of what and when, and regimented around the basics. From there, I rebuilt that schedule and myself.

That's the real work of boundaries: Not just protecting your energy, but redefining your life to match who you've become.

INSIGHTS TO CONSIDER:

1. Living on Purpose Requires Unlearning Survival Patterns

When you grow up in environments where chaos or unpre-dictability is normal, your nervous system adapts by prioritizing external demands over internal needs. This survival wiring can make boundaries feel unsafe, even selfish. But neuroscience shows that the brain and body *can* be rewired toward safety and intention through conscious repetition and rest.[1]

✧ Reflect: Is your "drive" rooted in purpose or protection?

2. Boundaries Aren't Just Emotional—They're Biological

Chronic overextension leads to dysregulation in your nervous system. Studies have shown that people who regularly override their limits experience higher cortisol levels, immune dysfunction, and emotional burnout. In contrast, setting boundaries helps recal-ibrate your internal stress response system.[2]

✧ Reflect: Every "no" you speak protects your body's "yes."

3. You Are Allowed to Redefine Success at Any Point

Success is not a static target; it's personal, contextual, and evolving. Research in positive psychology reveals that individuals who define success in terms of internal alignment (rather than status or comparison) tend to experience greater well-being, satisfaction, and sustainable motivation.[3]

✧ Reflect: What does success *feel* like in your body, not just on paper?

BEFORE YOU TURN THE PAGE...

This chapter was my story.

Now, I invite you to look at your own.

You may not be bedbound. You may not have a chronic illness. But I'll bet there are places in your life where you've said yes out of guilt, where you've ignored your body's whisper or clung to relationships or roles that no longer reflect who you are becoming.

Living on purpose doesn't require a crisis.

But sometimes, it takes one to remember what matters.

Take a breath. Take inventory.

You're allowed to make different choices now.

PAUSE AND REFLECT:

You're not selfish for setting boundaries.
You're wise for knowing your limits.

1. What beliefs have you outgrown that you're still living by?
2. Where are you saying yes out of habit or fear?
3. Who in your life supports the version of you that is becoming, not the one you've outgrown?
4. What boundary could you set that would bring you peace, not guilt?
5. Where are you spending energy that isn't aligned with your values?
6. When was the last time you listened to your body and responded with compassion?
7. What rhythms or routines could you shift to better support your well-being?
8. What are you afraid might happen if you slowed down?

ROOTED, NOT RUSHED

You don't owe anyone the version of you that made them comfortable.
You deserve a life that supports your healing, not just your survival.

Chapter 4
Soft Doesn't Mean Small

"I am not afraid of storms, for I am learning how to sail my ship."
—Louisa May Alcott

Somewhere along the way, I was taught that strength had to be hard, that being taken seriously meant staying polished and professional, that softness was weakness, that emotion was indulgent, that silence meant submission.

But healing unraveled all of that.

Because when your life slows down enough—either by choice or by force —you start to realize that so much of what you've carried wasn't truth, but conditioning.

I recall moments as a child when softness felt dangerous and tears were seen as weakness or hesitation as failure. I don't think anyone said it out loud, but I absorbed it anyway: To survive, you had to be tough.

Tenderness didn't earn protection; it invited judgment and negative physical attention.

So, I toughened up.

I learned to smile when I wanted to cry, to lead even when I felt lost, and in doing so, I buried the parts of me that longed to simply be held, understood, and allowed to rest. I had to unlearn the idea that my voice only mattered if it was in agreement and not out of line. To be respected, I had to perform with certainty, even when I was breaking inside.

Let me be clear: Softness isn't the easy route.

It takes enormous strength to respond with compassion when you're triggered.

It takes self-control to pause instead of defend.

It takes deep-rooted confidence to lead with kindness in a world that often confuses dominance with power.

But once you find your voice in softness, you begin to see that it doesn't make you small.

It makes you safe for yourself and for others.

What surprised me most was that when I let myself soften, I didn't disappear. I became clearer. I became stronger and truer.

I stopped explaining myself to people who didn't want to understand.

I stopped chasing relationships that required me to over-function.

I stopped shrinking to maintain the peace.

And here's the truth I live by now: **Soft doesn't mean small. Soft means sovereign.**

I can speak kindly and still be heard.

I can say no with grace and still mean it.

I can rest without guilt.

I can lead without burning out.

I can feel deeply and still move forward.

ROOTED, NOT RUSHED

This isn't a smaller version of me.

This is a more whole one.

My voice has changed. It's slower now and more intentional. Nothing I do anymore is without intention, because I no longer have the luxury of spending my energy carelessly.

Early on, I made an agreement with myself: If life turned out to be shorter than expected, I would live it as fully and honestly as I could, so I could leave this world knowing I showed up with love, purpose, and every ounce of my true self and heart.

And the more I healed emotionally, the more gratitude I started to feel.

I began to see people more clearly.

I felt things more deeply.

I carried a kind of love for the world that I don't think I could describe, even now. It's something you only understand when everything familiar has been stripped away and you're still here, breathing, noticing the light through the window like it's the first time you've really seen it.

As I fought to heal my body, I knew my world had to shift. There was too much love to be lost in a life spent chasing the wrong things.

So I started showing up differently.

It wasn't some polished transformation. It was survival. Before the speaking events, before clarity, I was just trying to keep living, even while sick. I wasn't always polished. I showed up without makeup, in any way I could muster.

But even then, I was living.

I was trying.

And in that rawness, my softness became my power.

It changed how I connect with clients, receive support, and build systems that protect my energy, peace, and purpose.

I remember sitting in a leadership meeting not long ago, and instead of pushing for fast answers or metrics, I paused.

I asked my team how they were really doing, not to tick a box, but because I genuinely cared.

That small question shifted the energy in the room. We ended up having one of the most honest and productive conversations we'd had in months. The results still got done, but the approach felt human.

That's what softness makes room for.

I used to think work was work, and life was life.

But now I know: The way you move through your life shapes the way you lead.

I used to fear softness in business.

I thought it meant being walked on.

And honestly, at one point, it did.

But now, I lead with softness and strength.

And because I've stopped hiding what I'm navigating, my team shows up differently, too.

We're more honest. We're more flexible. We communicate more clearly, support more intentionally, and solve problems without the emotional chaos.

We've built a different kind of culture, not by pretending everything's okay, but by learning how to lead from real life.

I still don't know what tomorrow looks like, but I'm no longer afraid of that uncertainty that comes with it. Because if I'm leading from truth, I'm leading from solid ground.

INSIGHTS TO CONSIDER:

1. Gentleness Is a Nervous System Strategy, Not a Weakness

Softness is often mislabeled as fragility, but from a neurobiological standpoint, cultivating calm, grounded responses is a sign of a well-regulated nervous system. Co-regulation (how we help others feel safe) begins with our internal sense of safety.[1]

✧ Reflect: When I soften, am I collapsing or grounding?

2. Quiet Leadership Creates Brave Spaces

Research in emotional intelligence and leadership shows that vulnerability and emotional attunement—hallmarks of "soft strength"—increase trust, team cohesion, and innovation. When leaders model genuine presence over performative perfection, they create a safe environment for others to do the same.[2]

✧ Reflect: Where can I lead from empathy instead of ego?

3. Strength Without Softness Often Becomes Armor

Toughness without tenderness can easily give rise to self-abandonment. True strength includes boundaries *and* emotional depth. It includes knowing when to pause, when to speak gently, and when to rest.[3]

✧ Reflect: Am I strong because I'm armored, or because I'm anchored?

BEFORE YOU TURN THE PAGE...

This chapter was my story.

Now, I invite you to look at your own.

Maybe you've been told your softness is a liability.

Maybe you've learned to stay small to avoid judgment, or to protect your space, or to be what others expect.

But here's what I know:

You don't have to be hardened to be strong.
You don't have to be loud to be heard.
You don't have to be fearless to be free.

Your softness is not weakness. It's *evidence* of all you've survived without letting it make you bitter.

Take a breath. Loosen the armor. Let yourself feel what's true.

PAUSE AND REFLECT:

1. **What have I been taught about strength, and is it still true for me?**

Where did I first learn it was safer to be polished than to be present?

2. **Where have I been quiet to protect others' comfort, and what has that cost me?**

What would it feel like to speak with honesty, even if it makes others uncomfortable?

3. Have I ever mistaken softness for weakness in myself or others?

What qualities do I now see as powerful that I used to dismiss?

4. How would my life feel different if I stopped performing and started leading from who I really am?

In business, relationships, and daily life, what would shift?

5. Where am I leading from fear, and what would it look like to lead from love instead?

What would change if I prioritized peace over perfection?

6. When was the last time I allowed rest without guilt?

What story am I still believing that says I have to earn my worth?

7. What boundaries could help protect my softness, not harden me further?

You're allowed to lead gently.
You're allowed to live slowly.
You're allowed to speak with kindness and still be heard.
Soft is not small. It's sacred.

Chapter 5
The In-Between Is Still Sacred

"You are not behind. You are exactly where you need to be.
Every moment is part of becoming."
—Brianna Wiest

We love a transformation story: the comeback, the glow-up, the clean arc where something challenging happens, a lesson is learned, and life becomes something better than it was before.

But real life doesn't move that neatly.

Most of it happens in the *in-between,* that strange, sacred space where you're no longer who you were, but not yet who you're becoming.

You've outgrown certain roles, routines, and relationships, but haven't quite figured out what fits yet. Healing isn't linear, clarity isn't immediate, and some days still bring you to your knees.

I've lived in that place longer than I ever expected.

And at first, it felt like failure.

I felt behind.

But eventually, I realized: The in-between isn't a delay.

It's the becoming.

It's the space where your roots deepen before your next growth.

Your silence speaks louder than any performance.

Your soul begins asking better questions, even if the answers take time.

It's the space where I learned how to sit with what hurt without rushing past it.

I learned how to hold joy and grief in the same hand.

I discovered that *not knowing what comes next* isn't a weakness; it's an invitation to trust myself differently.

As my health declined from 2020 onward, my business suffered. And while my ego sometimes wants to take credit—or blame—for all of it, the truth is more complex. It didn't fail, but it *did* have to change.

We were stretched thin. We fought to stay afloat through supply chain breakdowns, financial stressors, and a global shift that forced every decision to be more intentional.

I have often wondered what would've happened if I had been healthier. Could we have handled things differently? Held on to more? Expanded faster? How could I have been a better leader to change it (or try to control it)?

But I've come to believe that sometimes the universe doesn't just nudge you; it shakes you. When you're not learning from the lessons the gentle way, life will bring them louder.

That's what happened in our business.

We didn't fail, but we *restructured*.

We let go of some things. We reimagined others.

We shifted how we worked, how we supported each other, how we served our clients, and how we made space for real life behind the scenes.

Through those hardest years of illness, through COVID, and even before I had clear diagnoses, my business suffered. In 2023, I made the difficult decision to close one of my other ventures, my event planning business, just as it was beginning to take off, and COVID quarantine was no longer limiting events. Being sick meant I couldn't execute the full days required. When I really faced the reality that my body was sentencing me with, I simply let it go.

Success is not a straight line. It's a series of recalibrations. It's learning to adapt, evolve, and stretch without breaking.

Sometimes it's not about going back.

What I didn't realize at first was how lonely the in-between can feel. There's no arrival party and no applause. There are only quiet days where the milestones are invisible to others, but monumental to you.

For me, it looked like cooking my own dinner for the first time in weeks, or finishing a task without needing to lie down, or simply choosing joy even when grief still lingers.

Those are the moments that mark progress. But you have to learn how to celebrate yourself, even when no one else notices. That's part of the work, too.

Letting go wasn't just a business decision. It was a spiritual one. It meant releasing the version of myself who was always pushing, always performing, always trying to hold everything together.

In the stillness that followed, I started to meet the version of me I had never made space for:

The one who leads differently.

The one who trusts more.

The one who no longer needs to prove her value through overextension, because she has to choose what her body can bear.

And even now, I've hit ceilings I didn't expect.

I might look okay today, but the labels others carry about your past often linger longer than the truth of your present.

There's an invisible stigma to being sick.

People are waiting for you to break again.

Your today can't possibly be real, because they remember your yesterday.

But here's what changed everything for me: I stopped trying to explain it. I stopped trying to win back the imagination of people who couldn't see me now. And I started rebuilding, not the old version of my life, but a new one. This new life was one I imagined from the ground up.

I rewrote my schedule.

I redefined my habits.

I re-evaluated how I want to *feel* while working, living, and leading.

I'm not back in the gym: My capacity still fluctuates, and my energy has limits I've learned to respect. But I don't move now to change my body. I move to *retrain* it, restore the connection, and build capacity.

And that's what this season has been about: a complete reimagining of the life I want to live and the person I want to be while living it, because every day I choose to keep going *is a step toward something better.*

INSIGHTS TO CONSIDER:

1. Liminal Space Is Where Identity Rewrites Itself

Liminality—a term used in psychology and anthropology—refers to that "in-between" place where we are no longer who we were, but not yet who we're becoming. It often feels directionless or disorienting, but it is also where transformation happens most profoundly.[1]

✧ Reflect: Am I rushing through the in-between or allowing it to reshape me?

2. Resilience Looks Like Staying, Not Sprinting

One of the greatest acts of resilience is staying present in the face of uncertainty. Studies in trauma recovery and post-traumatic growth show that learning to tolerate ambiguity is linked to stronger long-term well-being, deeper self-awareness, and healthier decision-making.[2]

✧ Reflect: What have I learned from not knowing and still continuing?

3. Letting Go Creates Space for Renewal

The act of surrendering—to what's gone, no longer working, or no longer fits—can feel like failure. However, in reality, it creates the mental, emotional, and even physical space required for a new vision, deeper alignment, and a clearer future.[3]

✧ Reflect: What have I let go of that made room for something better?

BEFORE YOU TURN THE PAGE...

This chapter was my story.

Now, I invite you to look at your own.

Maybe you're standing in a life that doesn't look like what you hoped.

Maybe you've let go of things you never expected to lose.

Maybe you're rebuilding something quietly, still unsure of what it will become.

That doesn't mean you've failed.

It means you're still becoming.

This in-between?

It's not the absence of a future.

It's the foundation of it.

You're not behind.

You're *becoming*.

PAUSE AND REFLECT:

**The middle isn't meaningless.
It's where your truest self is shaped.**

I. **What have I lost or let go of that still carries grief?**

Give yourself permission to name what didn't go the way you planned. There's no shame in mourning what might have been.

2. **What is quietly growing in my life, even if I haven't seen the full bloom yet?**

    Look for small signs of strength, softness, or clarity that have taken root in you.

3. **Am I trying to get "back to normal," or am I ready to imagine something better?**

    Where am I looking backward out of habit instead of forward with intention?

4. **What daily habit, thought, or choice could help rebuild the life I want to live, one small step at a time?**

    Progress doesn't always look like motion. Sometimes it's simply staying present.

5. **Who am I becoming, even if no one else sees it yet?**

    Let yourself answer without apology.

6. **What expectations am I still holding that are quietly weighing me down?**

    What if letting go is what sets me free?

You're not lost. You're becoming.
The in-between isn't a pause. It's a path.
Honor your becoming, even before it makes sense.

Chapter 6
The Body Keeps the Wisdom

"The body keeps the score. If the memory of trauma is encoded in the viscera, in heartbeats and gut-wrenching sensations... then we must also include the body in healing."
—Bessel van der Kolk

I used to think my body had turned against me.

It betrayed me.

It broke down at the worst possible time.

It couldn't keep up with the life I was fighting to maintain.

But now, I see it differently.

My body wasn't failing me. It was communicating in the only language it had left. And because I didn't know how to listen, it had to speak louder.

For years before diagnosis, I had ignored what my body tried to whisper. I masked the pain and pushed through symptoms that had followed me since childhood—my mom used to say I always came home "sickly" after visiting my dad. Even after being diagnosed with celiac disease in 2004, I brushed off the signs, adapting and coping until everything came to a halt in 2020.

The tension in my chest told me I was pushing too hard.

Nausea flared when I was around people who drained me.

Headaches, fatigue, and subtle but consistent signs told me I had been living *outside myself* for too long.

But I was too busy being "on."

∾

And so, my faithful and wise body did what it knew to do. It kept the score. It held the pain.

It stored the trauma, stress, and shame in places I didn't even know to check, until eventually, it couldn't anymore.

At first, I thought it was all random: the panic attacks, nausea that came out of nowhere, muscle tension, racing heart, and days when I couldn't eat or speak or even think straight.

But when I started asking questions, I learned something that changed everything: **The body remembers what the mind tries to survive.**

Trauma doesn't just live in your memories. It lives in your nervous system, your muscles, your gut, your lungs, and your sleep. And when your body doesn't feel safe, it doesn't need your permission to shut everything down.

It just does.

Here's a little truth you should know: When you go through something traumatic or live in a state of chronic stress, your nervous system adapts. It goes into fight, flight, freeze, or fawn—sometimes for moments, sometimes for years.

And the longer you stay in that mode, the harder it becomes to return to rest.

Over time, your body learns to associate even *everyday life* with danger: lights, emails, demands, conversations.

Your body is doing exactly what it was designed to do: **protect you.** But protection isn't peace.

The **vagus nerve**, a key messenger between your brain and body, plays a significant role in stress response and digestion. When overstimulated, it can create symptoms like fainting, heart palpitations, and even shutdown.

Chronic stress and trauma **rewire** your brain's survival pathways, making it hard to tell the difference between an actual threat and a subtle trigger.

Emotional pain doesn't just sit in your heart. It settles in your gut, joints, posture, and breathing.

So no, it wasn't "all in my head," and it wasn't my body being dramatic or disobedient.

It was my body doing the only thing it knew to do after years of not being heard: **speaking louder.**

The moment I realized my health issues were rooted in a lifetime of chronic stress was a turning point.

It was the moment I stopped asking, *Why is my body doing this to me?* and started asking, *What is my body trying to say?*

That small, quiet, but powerful shift began to change everything.

I started treating my body like it wasn't the problem.

I started seeing it as my partner, my messenger, and my mirror.

Before that shift, I treated my body like a machine—something to push and override. I ignored hunger. I minimized exhaustion. I wore pain like it was a badge of honor, because that's what I thought strength looked like.

But real strength isn't in the override. It's in the quiet noticing. Stop and ask, *What am I needing right now?* That's when everything started to change, not just in how I felt, but in who I became.

When I started working *with* my body—through food, breath, movement, and silence—healing came from learning to listen. And when I finally started *really listening*, I began to see everything in a different light.

I look at pictures now, and I notice the signs I missed. I see the **moon face**, round with inflammation, which I didn't recognize at the time. I just smiled through it, covered it with makeup, and tried to look "normal."

I remember the **chronic pain** in my neck, back, and legs— all of which I attributed to the wrong reasons. I blamed the bad chair, the long day, and the stress. Not once did I stop to think, *Maybe this isn't just circumstantial. Maybe this is systemic.*

My **blood pressure** was 200 over 150, over and over again.

It wasn't just anxiety.

It wasn't just a "moment."

It was my body waving a red flag I didn't know how to interpret.

Even the **emotional flare-ups**—the moments I felt like shutting down, withdrawing, or escaping—weren't random either. They weren't character flaws. They were responses.

And the isolation I felt during that season? It was biological: hormonal, neurological, and physical.

What felt like a dozen separate struggles were never separate at all. And that's what trauma does. It fragments the body, mind, and memory until you begin to believe it's all isolated.

But healing is what brings the pieces back together.

It's the moment when the pain, fatigue, anxiety, inflammation, and shutdowns stop feeling like symptoms to manage and start revealing themselves as **messages to be honored.**

When I started to understand that my body wasn't the enemy, but the narrator of everything I had lived through, I stopped trying to "fix" it and started trying to *hear* it.

And slowly, the way I showed up changed.

ROOTED, NOT RUSHED

I stopped rushing through mornings.

I gave my body time to wake up.

I took my medications with presence, not resentment.

I breathed on purpose.

I rested when the first whisper of fatigue came, not when it screamed.

I ate not just to fuel, but to **respect** the parts of me that were still fighting to keep me here.

I hydrated like it was a promise.

Rebuilding trust with my body wasn't instant. It wasn't like flipping a switch and suddenly feeling whole. Some days, I still doubted what I felt. I second-guessed what I needed. But each small act of care—each glass of water, each slow breath, each time I chose presence over punishment— began rewriting that relationship.

I wasn't just learning to listen.

I was learning to trust myself again.

I created rhythms, not routines—gentle anchors I could return to when the world felt like too much.

I no longer moved my body to "earn" anything; I moved to *return* to myself.

And still, there were days I couldn't leave my bed. Walking to the front door felt like climbing a mountain. The fatigue was so thick, I didn't know where my strength had gone.

And on those days, I reminded myself:

This, too, is part of healing.

This, too, counts.

This, too, is enough.

There were still hard moments when the pain took over, and I wanted to push through just like before. But I knew better now. And when you know better, you *tend* better.

So I stopped asking for perfection and started offering partnership.

That, for me, was when healing began.

INSIGHTS TO CONSIDER:

1. Your Body Is Wired for Survival—and for Healing

The autonomic nervous system (ANS), which regulates involuntary bodily functions such as heart rate and digestion, has two main branches: the sympathetic ("fight or flight") and the parasympathetic ("rest and repair"). When stress is prolonged, we stay stuck in survival mode, but with time and support, the body can relearn how to feel safe.[1]

✧ Reflect: What helps my body feel safe, physically and emotionally?

2. Emotions Are Felt in the Body, Not Just the Mind

Research shows that unprocessed emotions (grief, anger, fear) are stored in the body as tension, inflammation, and disconnection. This doesn't mean you're broken. It means your body remembers, and it's asking you to pay attention.[2]

✧ Reflect: Where do I carry my stress or sadness physically? What happens when I notice it with compassion?

3. Gentle Consistency Rebuilds Safety Over Time

Healing isn't about doing "everything right." It's about rebuilding a sense of internal safety through small, consistent cues: breathing slowly, honoring your limits, choosing nourishment, and establishing a routine. These aren't weaknesses; they're anchors.[3]

✧ Reflect: What small practice helps me return to myself, even when things feel chaotic?

PAUSE AND REFLECT:

Your body isn't working against you.

It's trying to speak to you.

Will you listen?

1. What physical signals have I been brushing off, minimizing, or powering through?

What would it look like to pause instead of push?

2. When does my body feel safe?

Are there environments, people, or practices that allow me to soften and breathe?

3. How has my body been asking for rhythm, nourishment, or rest, and how have I responded?

What's one slight shift I can make in partnership with it?

4. What's a moment from my past where I now realize my body was asking for something different?

What might it have needed?

5. What would it feel like to treat my body as wise, not something to fix, fight, or fear?

What would change if I moved through my day with that in mind?

6. What is one act of care, today, that I can offer this body that's carried me through so much?

A breath, a kind thought, a slower pace, a stretch, or something else?

Your body is not your enemy. It's your home.
And when you start listening, it begins to heal.

Chapter 7
The Grief No One Talks About

"When we deny our stories, they define us.
When we own our stories, we get to write the ending."
—Brené Brown

Between 2020 and 2024, there were moments at the height of my illness when I grieved quietly, scrolling through someone else's milestones: birthday parties, retreats, business launches, and family trips.

Smiling faces and filtered captions made me feel like the world had kept spinning without me.

And in a way, it had.

I was watching life go on from the sidelines—still here, but not quite *in it,* not in the way I used to be.

That's a grief few people talk about: when you're not gone, but you're not included either. I grieved the memories I didn't get to make, the years when survival was the only goal.

I grieved the traditions I used to lead and the chaos I once orchestrated, now happening without me. I wasn't forgotten, but I wasn't central anymore. And that ache stayed, long after the decorations came down.

Holidays that once meant joyful chaos, handmade traditions, and creative entertaining were now replaced by watching others serve me or hearing the laughter from the other room while I rested in bed, trying to conserve energy.

I grieved the energy I used to spend so freely, when I could say yes without second-guessing what it would cost me.

And I grieved how easy it is for others to forget you're still navigating all of this, long after the crisis has passed.

But what I've learned in the ache is this: **Grief doesn't mean you're broken. It means something mattered.**

And learning to live with that grief—not ignore it, not rush it, but live *with* it—is one of the bravest things I've ever done. Because once I stopped trying to get "over it," I started learning how to move *with it,* with grace, permission, and, slowly, peace.

Letting go wasn't giving up: It was choosing to live differently.

And that choice, *every day*, is a form of resilience.

Resilience isn't always bold or loud. Sometimes it looks like tears on the bathroom floor, followed by a deep breath and a simple decision: *I'll try again tomorrow.*

Sometimes, it looks like walking away from a dream you outgrew, or finally admitting that something hurt more than you let on.

Some griefs aren't tied to one moment.

They're the slow erosion of what used to come easily.

The effortless laugh that now takes energy.

The ability to be spontaneous without a strategy.

The invitations that stop coming, not out of malice, but out of misunder-standing.

These are the quiet griefs no one warns you about.

The kind you carry in silence, and mourn in fragments.

And still, you carry on.

Resilience is the courage to keep becoming, even when the outcome is uncertain.

It's what lives in the middle of your grief.

It's not the opposite of pain.

It's what grows *inside* it.

This kind of resilience lives in all of us, within every broken expectation, missed opportunity, and quiet moment you wanted to give up but didn't.

I'm not who I used to be. I'm still grieving parts of her, but I'm also still here. And that means there's more to write.

And maybe that's what grief truly is: proof that you were present, that you loved something enough to miss it.

That belief and depth of care are part of becoming, too.

INSIGHTS TO CONSIDER:

1. Grief Isn't Just About Loss

Grief can be a quiet companion that lingers in unmet expectations, unspoken goodbyes, and unacknowledged change. It doesn't always announce itself with tears or dramatic moments; it can settle into the body and mind as a quiet ache or lingering thought.[1]

✧ Reflect: What is the quiet grief I've carried that hasn't had space to be acknowledged? How does it show up in my life?

2. The Power of Silent Resilience

Sometimes resilience isn't about big, heroic moments of bouncing back. It's about showing up when no one is watching, continuing even when it feels impossible, and carrying grief with quiet strength.[2]

✧ Reflect: In what quiet ways have I continued, even when it felt like I couldn't go on? How does resilience look in my day-to-day life?

3. Healing Grief Means Making Space for the Unfinished

Grief often doesn't have a clear ending—it doesn't always conclude with a neatly tied bow. Healing is less about "getting over it" and more about learning to live with the loss while allowing yourself to rebuild and grow.[3]

✧ Reflect: How have I made space for grief in my life without rushing to "fix" it? What's been the hardest part of living with loss?

BEFORE YOU TURN THE PAGE…

This chapter was my story.

Now, I invite you to look at your own.

Maybe your grief isn't loud or obvious.

Maybe it's the slow, quiet ache of what never happened.

The job that didn't pan out.

The relationship that unraveled.

The version of you that never got the chance to exist.

Maybe it's not just about what you've lost, but who you've had to become in the process.

Grief doesn't always announce itself.
But it always deserves to be honored.

And in the middle of that grief?

Resilience lives as the quiet choice to keep showing up

and keep becoming.

PAUSE AND REFLECT:

Resilience isn't what happens after grief.
It's what rises *through* it.

I. **What part of my story am I still grieving, even if it looks "small" from the outside?**

Let yourself name the loss, the shift, or the ache that still lives in you.

2. Where have I shown up—tired, tender, and uncertain—but still present?

This is what quiet strength looks like. Recognize it.

3. What have I let go of that once defined me?

And what space might that be creating for something new?

4. Have I been waiting to feel "ready" before I begin again?

What if I don't need to be ready, just *willing*?

5. What does resilience look like for me today, not as a concept, but as a choice?

Think small. Think simple. Think honestly.

You don't have to bounce back.
You're allowed to build forward.
Even if you're grieving.
Even if you're still healing.
Even if you're unsure.
You're already resilient.
Because you're still here, still soft, still becoming, still choosing life.

Chapter 8
The Courage to Be Seen

*"Owning our story and loving ourselves through
that process is the bravest thing we'll ever do."*
—Brené Brown

For a long time, I didn't want to be seen—not really.

I let people see what was polished, useful, and easy to digest.

I showed up strong. I smiled through discomfort. I let my accomplishments speak, so I didn't have to. But deep down, I was afraid that if people really saw my pain and uncertainty, I would be too much or not enough—or both.

And so I stayed small.

I edited myself in conversations. I second-guessed my opinions. I kept parts of my story in shadow because I didn't want the weight of misunderstanding.

But what I've learned is this: There is no healing in hiding.

The longer I kept trying to perform *perfection*, the further I drifted from peace. And eventually, I reached a point where I realized: I don't want to be invisible in my own life anymore. Visibility isn't about being flashy. It's not about the spotlight or praise. It's about ownership. It's about showing up in your life as the main character, not the supporting role.

Because for so long, it wasn't safe to use my voice.

As a child, I learned early: Words could be twisted. Truth could be ignored. What I said only mattered if it served them. So I silenced myself and hid in closets—sometimes literally, sometimes mentally.

I became proficient at speaking in a way that others wanted to hear me. My voice became a mirror that reflected their needs, not my own.

But at fourteen, something shifted. I saw the truth for what it was. I spoke out about the abuse.

That moment was the beginning of my voice becoming mine. It wasn't perfect. It didn't heal everything overnight, but it planted the seed that I had the right to speak for myself.

Years later, I found myself facing another moment where my voice had to fight to be heard.

In business, I was dismissed by a company that chose to engage only with my husband, despite having equal experience, equal ownership, and a deeply rooted presence in our field. I had been building, negotiating, and leading long before that moment, yet suddenly, my presence was treated like an accessory. I had let him be the mouthpiece for both of our work for too long, and now I was invisible to them.

They ignored me.

I allowed it for some time to maintain peace, thinking it would ensure a consistent and successful relationship between our organization and theirs, until I was forced to fight for my voice and my own earned respect.

I spoke. I brought proof. I took legal action. I stood in my truth with a steady hand.

And in the end, they backed down. They apologized.

ROOTED, NOT RUSHED

A press release of revision and change was posted.

I was finally seen as an equal co-founder—someone whose place and respect within the organization had been earned, not granted out of courtesy. I had just been too quiet for too long. And while that victory felt validating, it wasn't what gave me worth. I didn't find my voice in that moment. I proved that it had been there all along.

I realized that speaking up might not always be easy, but it's powerful.

For years, I let others narrate my story. I showed up to do the work, but I stepped back when it came time to claim it. I deferred. I deflected. I downplayed. And somewhere in that cycle, I forgot that I belonged to myself.

Speaking up wasn't just about being heard; it was about being whole. That's when the shift began. I started speaking my truth more often, even when my voice shook. I started saying what I meant, not just what I thought people wanted to hear. I stopped performing and started presenting myself as I am: soft-spoken, intentional, still becoming, but present.

That was the bravest thing I'd done yet.

Speaking up has never been easy for me. Even now, with all the growth, all the healing, there are still moments when my throat tightens, when my heart beats faster before I speak. Even now, there are moments when my voice trembles, when the room feels heavy with history, and I hear the echo of old messages telling me to be quiet, be small, be agreeable.

But the difference now? I don't confuse fear with failure.

I know that the voice shaking is still mine.

I speak anyway.

And every time I do, I reclaim a little more of myself.

INSIGHTS TO CONSIDER:

1. The Strength in Vulnerability

Showing up as you are is one of the strongest things you can do. Vulnerability doesn't make you weak; it makes you real. Being genuine is what builds connection and true resilience.[1]

✧ Reflect: In what ways have I avoided being seen in my authenticity? How can I embrace vulnerability as a source of strength?

2. Your Voice Is Your Power

It's not about being loud or assertive; it's about owning your voice and your truth. When you start speaking from a place of authenticity, others begin to listen, and you reclaim the power you've always had.[2]

✧ Reflect: Where in my life have I silenced my voice? What would it look like to speak my truth, even if it's uncomfortable?

3. The Freedom of Letting Go of Others' Expectations

We often shrink ourselves or hide our truth in fear of disappointing others or failing to meet their expectations. But the real freedom comes from realizing that you are enough as you are—no approval needed.[3]

✧ Reflect: Where am I still holding onto the weight of others' expectations? How would my life shift if I let go of that burden?

4. The Power of Owning Your Story

When you choose to embrace and own your story—both the light and the dark—it becomes your source of strength. No one can take that power from you. It is yours, and it shapes how you lead and live.[4]

✧ Reflect: How have I allowed my past to define me? What would it look like to reclaim my story on my terms?

BEFORE YOU TURN THE PAGE...

This chapter was my story.

Now, I invite you to look at your own.

You may not have fought a legal battle.

You may not have stood on a stage or told your story publicly.

But I'd bet there's a part of you that's still learning how to speak freely.

To be fully seen, not just for what you do, but for *who you are.*

Speaking up takes courage.

But hiding takes a toll, too.

And you don't have to stay small to stay safe anymore.

PAUSE AND REFLECT:

**Your voice doesn't need to be loud to be powerful.
It just needs to be *yours*.**

1. Where have I been holding back my truth out of fear of being misunderstood or dismissed?

What am I afraid might happen if I speak honestly?

2. What past experience taught me to silence myself?

Am I still living by that old rule, even now?

3. Who do I feel fully seen by, and what is it about their presence that makes space for my voice?

How can I give that gift to myself more often?

4. What have I accomplished, led, or carried that no one else knows about?

Let yourself *own* your role in the story.

5. What would I say if I weren't trying to be polite, perfect, or palatable?

Write it. Speak it. Let it rise.

You don't have to scream to be heard.
You just have to stop hiding.
You're not too much. You're not too little.
You're just finally letting yourself be seen.
Your voice matters because *you* do.

Chapter 9
Success, Redefined

"Don't aim for success if you want it; just do what you
love and believe in, and it will come naturally."
—David Frost

For a long time, I thought success meant being impressive.

I measured it in recognition, revenue, milestones, and how many people said "wow" when I told them what I did. And truthfully? I was good at it. I knew how to build, produce, deliver, and lead.

But behind the scenes, the version of me chasing all that success was also exhausted, overextended, and under-nourished in ways that had nothing to do with food.

I kept thinking the next win would fix the fatigue, that being seen would make me feel whole.

But it didn't. Because what I was really craving wasn't praise. It was *peace*.

And when my health crashed, when life stripped away the schedule and the status and the public-facing shine, I had to ask myself a hard question: *If I couldn't be impressive anymore, would I still feel valuable?*

Starting in 2020, during the long days, I was too sick to move and unable to even leave my bed, listening to the quiet hum of the house around me, everything began to shift. The silence felt cruel at first, until it became a question I couldn't avoid: Who am I without the "doing"?

I realized I didn't want success that costs me myself.

I wanted success that aligned with my values.

I wanted success that left room for my body, my joy, and my actual life.

I wanted success that I could feel, not just perform.

And it turns out that kind of success feels *very* different than what I was taught to chase.

Success isn't just the hustle anymore. It's not the late-night emails, the packed calendar, the highlight reel. For me, success has become something much more personal: something softer, slower, and truer.

I used to think slowing down meant losing ground. If I weren't running full speed, someone else would pass me.

But now I see that real growth isn't always loud. It doesn't need to be broadcast to be valid.

It's the kind of growth that's rooted, that strengthens before it shows. It's the power of the tree that didn't bloom overnight, but grew quietly, consistently, with intention.

That's the kind of success I want now—one with roots, not just reach.

What I once considered successful now feels heavy and measured against someone else's scale. I used to think I had to keep achieving just to keep up, but I've learned that moving slower doesn't mean I'm falling behind.

It means I'm *present*. It means I'm paying attention to the process, not just the prize.

And strangely, this slower success feels more meaningful.

I can actually enjoy it.

I've stopped measuring success by what I give. I used to chase validation like it was currency: a good review, a public win, a compliment I didn't ask for—those were the markers.

But lately, the wins I celebrate are different: saying no to something that doesn't align, resting before I burn out, making a decision that no one sees, but that honors the version of me I've fought to become. These don't show up on spreadsheets, but they're the evidence of a life well-lived.

I no longer chase success for status. I seek success that includes **safety**, emotionally, physically, and spiritually.

I've learned that life will knock you down. That's not failure.

Real success is how you *rise,* how you meet the fall with curiosity instead of shame, and how you let yourself grow in the space where you once would've given up.

I don't just see achievements anymore; I see *growth.*

I see every hard lesson as an invitation.

Every challenge is a chance to come home to myself.

Every small win is something worth celebrating.

Success used to mean proving myself; now it means *knowing myself and honoring that person every day.*

And there's one more truth I've come to learn: For years, I carried a tension toward the idea of competition. In an industry built on rankings, performance, and constant measurement, I developed a quiet resistance that told me I had to be better, faster, more.

I thought that mindset kept me sharp, but it really kept me guarded. I wasn't collaborating. I was comparing. And comparison doesn't make you stronger. It just makes you suspicious.

I saw competitors as threats, not as people just trying to do the same thing I was: *make it.*

But recently, I caught myself noticing a competitor's sign on the road. Instead of that old, tight urge to outperform, I smiled.

I thought, *We're both still in the game.*

And that felt like freedom.

I don't need to tear anyone down to build something great; I don't have to operate from scarcity to feel strong; I don't have to compare what one is doing to my own success; *I don't have to outperform to belong.*

I can root for others and still rise.

Because now, I know: **There's room for all of us.**

INSIGHTS TO CONSIDER:

1. Redefining Success: Moving from External Validation to Internal Fulfillment

Success is often tied to external markers such as wealth, recognition, or status. However, true success is about aligning with your values, achieving fulfillment, and the impact you have on both others and yourself.[1]

✧ Reflect: What external markers of success have I chased in the past? How can I redefine success to align with what truly fulfills me?

2. The Role of Rest in Success

We live in a culture that often equates success with busyness and hustle. But rest is essential for growth, clarity, and long-term success. It's through rest that we regenerate our energy, creativity, and ability to lead.[2]

✧ Reflect: How do I view rest in my life? What would happen if I started treating rest as a crucial part of my success?

3. The Power of Saying No to Say Yes to What Matters

Saying no isn't just about avoiding things—it's about saying yes to the things that align with your values. By setting boundaries and protecting your energy, you create space for what truly matters.[3]

✧ Reflect: Where am I still saying yes out of obligation instead of alignment? How can I practice saying no to make space for what truly matters?

4. Success Isn't About Perfection—It's About Progress

So often we believe success means achieving something perfectly, but real success is found in the small steps we take every day toward progress. It's in how we navigate setbacks, learn, and continue moving forward.[4]

✧ Reflect: What are the small, consistent actions that contribute to my success? How can I celebrate progress rather than focusing on perfection?

5. Shifting From Comparison to Collaboration

In the past, you might have measured your success by comparing yourself to others. But true success comes from collaboration, not competition. There's space for everyone to thrive, and we all rise when we lift each other up.[5]

✧ Reflect: How has comparison impacted my success? What would it look like to focus more on collaboration and mutual growth?

BEFORE YOU TURN THE PAGE...

This chapter was my story.

Now, I invite you to look at your own.

Maybe you've spent years measuring your worth by output, what others think, how fast you move, or how much you produce.

Maybe you've felt the pressure to compete, prove, and constantly do more.

Maybe the ego kept you going, but also kept you blind to the real truth.

But what if success isn't in the sprint?

What if it's in the quiet courage to define success on your terms, without having to overprove yourself?

What if it's not about climbing higher, but going deeper?

PAUSE AND REFLECT:

Success isn't a title.
It's how your life *feels*.
And you get to choose the meaning behind the wins.

1. How have I defined success up until now, and whose version of success have I been chasing?

Be honest. Where did those expectations come from?

2. What if success wasn't about output but about alignment?

What would change in how I spend my time or lead others?

3. What is my relationship with competition?

Does it energize me, exhaust me, or disconnect me from my purpose?

4. When do I feel most at peace in my work or personal life?

Let that be a marker—not a reward, but a *guide.*

5. What version of success would feel like *freedom* for me?

What would it look like, and what would it take to create it?

You don't need to win someone else's race.
You just need to build a life that feels like yours.
And if it feels like peace, it might already be success.
Let peace be your proof.
Let alignment and authenticity be your arrival.
Let success feel like freedom.

Chapter 10
The Power of Saying No

"You can be a good person with a kind heart and still say no."
—Lori Deschene

I didn't know I needed support until it was too late.

I had been saying yes for so long—out of habit, guilt, and fear—that I forgot how to say no without a lengthy explanation or apology.

And deep down, I was afraid of what would happen if I stopped showing up for everyone else.

Would they still love me?

Would they stay?

Would they understand?

When my health crashed, I was forced into boundaries I had never given myself before.

My body said no before my voice ever did.

I couldn't over-function.

I couldn't people-please.

I couldn't keep the same pace.

And at first, that felt like failure, but now I see it was a turning point.

For me, that turning point happened during those hard years after 2020, when I had to start saying no to things I would have forced myself to do before: meetings, projects, even social events. I learned to put rest on my calendar like an appointment, to pause before saying yes, and to trust that people who truly loved me would understand. It wasn't just work—it was even friendships that couldn't hold space for my limits. It was messy and painful and real, but it taught me that my body would say no for me if I didn't listen.

I learned that no is not a rejection. It's a recognition of what my life can hold, and it doesn't mean I love people any less. It means I've finally learned how to love myself, too.

I used to think saying no meant closing a door.

Now I know it opens the ones that matter.

When I stopped saying yes to everything, I made space for what truly aligns: rest, peace, and truthful relationships that don't depend on me constantly overextending.

I've learned that if someone only values me for what I can give them, then their love was never love. It was access.

Boundaries showed me that I'm still generous, just not at the cost of myself. Saying no helped me find my yes again: yes to what matters, to where I thrive, to the kind of connection that doesn't drain me.

And what surprised me most? The world didn't fall apart when I stopped saying yes to everything.

But I stopped falling apart.

I became more grounded, honest, and whole.

ROOTED, NOT RUSHED

More honest.

More whole.

Now, no is a full sentence. And sometimes it's the most loving word I know.

Not everyone understood when I started saying no. Some people pulled away. Some were confused. Others assumed I was just being difficult, or distant, or different.

And the truth is, I *was* different.

I was no longer available in the same ways, over-explained my limits, or rushed in to save everyone while quietly burning myself out.

It wasn't always graceful. There were awkward conversations, missed invites, and misunderstandings.

But the relationships that mattered adjusted. They respected the space I created and even began creating their own.

And in that shift, I discovered something I never expected: Boundaries don't just protect; they invite.

They invite clarity and peace. They ask the right kind of people to stay, and the wrong ones to walk away.

Saying no was never about shutting people out; it was about setting boundaries.

It was about finally letting myself in.

Now, I don't say no because I'm angry, or closed off, or bitter.

I say no because I'm clear.

I say no because I'm healing.

I say no because I want my yes to mean something.

And maybe that's the biggest shift of all: Learning that my boundaries don't make me selfish. They make me sustainable.

INSIGHTS TO CONSIDER:

1. The Power of Boundaries: Protecting Your Energy

Setting boundaries isn't about pushing people away, but about making sure that what comes into your life aligns with your needs and values. Boundaries empower you to say yes to what truly matters while saying no to what drains you.[1]

✧ Reflect: What are my most essential boundaries? How can I strengthen them to protect my time, energy, and peace?

2. No as an Act of Self-Love

Learning to say no is one of the most compassionate things you can do for yourself. It's not rejection of others, but a recognition of your capacity and well-being. Saying no allows you to honor yourself without guilt.[2]

✧ Reflect: How have I been afraid to say no? What would happen if I said no more often for the sake of my own well-being?

3. The Guilt That Comes with Saying No

We often associate saying no with guilt, especially if we fear disappointing others. But guilt is a sign that you're prioritizing others over yourself, which is unsustainable in the long run.[3]

✧ Reflect: What kinds of guilt do I feel when I say no? How can I let go of guilt and honor my own needs without feeling bad?

4. Saying No as a Way to Say Yes to What Matters

Every time you say no to something that doesn't serve you, you're saying yes to something that does. Saying no creates space for the opportunities, people, and experiences that truly align with your goals and values.[4]

✧ Reflect: What opportunities am I creating by saying no to things that don't serve me? What is the "yes" I'm making space for?

5. Boundaries and Self-Respect

Establishing boundaries isn't just about protecting yourself; it's also about respecting yourself enough to recognize when something isn't serving you. Boundaries reflect your self-worth and communicate to others how they should treat you.[5]

✧ Reflect: What boundaries do I need to establish to respect myself and my time more? How can I communicate those boundaries with confidence?

BEFORE YOU TURN THE PAGE…

This chapter was my story.

Now, I invite you to look at your own.

Have you ever said yes when your soul was screaming no?

Have you ever kept showing up—exhausted, resentful, or afraid to disappoint—just to hold everything together?

What if the most loving thing you could do for yourself and your people was to *stop*?

PAUSE AND REFLECT:

A boundary isn't a wall.
It's a doorway into a more honest life.

1. What have I been saying yes to that's no longer aligned with who I am or how I want to live?

Where am I giving out of guilt instead of joy?

2. Where have I ignored my limits out of fear of what others might think?

And how has that impacted my health, energy, or peace?

3. What relationships feel lighter when I'm honest about my needs?

What shifted when I stopped over-functioning?

4. What would it feel like to say no without apology?

Where might that open space be for more meaningful yeses?

5. What boundary is my life asking me to set right now?

And what kind of freedom might come from honoring it?

You are allowed to disappoint others to honor yourself.
You are allowed to rest without earning it.
You are allowed to say no and still be deeply loved.

Chapter 11
Faith in the Fog

"Faith is taking the first step even when you
don't see the whole staircase."
—Martin Luther King Jr

It came in the middle of the night, through a sermon on TV. The message repeated itself again and again in unexpected places. One word kept coming back to me like a whisper: "Empowered."

That night, something in my spirit stood up. I stopped asking, *Why me?* and started asking, *What now?*

2023 became the year everything quietly changed.

It wasn't because I was healed, but because something inside me shifted. I had reached a depth I didn't want to return to. My thoughts had grown darker and heavier. And though I never made a plan, I had moments when I asked myself if I could really keep living like "this."

But deep down, I knew I wasn't a quitter. I just didn't know how much more I could take.

That was the moment I had to decide:

Would I give up or give in?

For years, I had been holding on tightly to control and to the idea that if I could just do enough, try enough, pray enough, something would finally click. But it wasn't until I let go of needing to make sense of it all that something else stepped in.

I used to think faith had to be unwavering, that if I had questions, I wasn't faithful enough.

But now I know that genuine faith isn't the absence of doubt—it's the willingness to keep choosing hope *even in its presence*.

Some of the most faithful things I've ever done didn't look like church pews or perfect prayers.

They looked like breathing through panic and saying, "I don't know how, but I trust You do."

Faith isn't perfect, but it's persistent.

That was the year I stopped holding on and finally let something greater hold me.

Now let me be clear on this: My translation of faith is within my love for my faithful Father and Jesus Christ. For others, that same faith may relate better to your spirituality of what or whom resonates with you. This is not for me to tell you what your faith should be or what you call that higher being. This is simply to share with you how faith sits within me. But faith gives us purpose, and that is where the sacred empowerment is found.

Empowerment didn't mean I suddenly had energy. It didn't come because I was healed or healing. I spent time not committing to anything in fear that I couldn't predict if I could show up or follow through.

But now, empowered in a new light, I finally stopped waiting for perfect circumstances to start *participating* in my life again.

The shift came in speaking to myself differently.

Empowerment meant honoring my capacity without guilt, letting rest be productive, and permitting myself to rebuild at a pace that didn't break me.

I started seeing evidence of peace.

I started speaking up again. I set boundaries that didn't come with over-explanations. I said no without spiraling. I said yes to what I knew was right, even if it made others uncomfortable.

And most of all, I began to feel trust in my spirit again—not just in God, but in me.

I stopped second-guessing every decision.

I stopped editing myself to keep the peace.

I stopped pretending I wasn't still healing.

My life didn't magically fix itself, but the pressure I had put on myself to carry it all *lifted*.

There were moments I felt alone in my faith, not because God had left me, but because I couldn't always explain what I was carrying. People wanted the update—the praise report, the miracle.

But I was still in the middle. And I didn't have the words to say, "I'm trusting, but I'm also tired."

That's the kind of faith no one claps for: the faith that lives in hospital rooms, late-night cries, and unanswered prayers.

But even then, I wasn't without grace. I was still held.

Empowerment became less about strength and more about surrender. It meant I could be uncertain and still be faithful, broken and still valuable, in progress and still worthy of peace.

For me, faith didn't show up as loud declarations or perfect belief.

It showed up in small, sacred ways, especially on the days I didn't feel strong.

It looked like whispering a prayer in the dark, even when I wasn't sure what I was asking for.

It looked like playing worship music in the background while I cleaned or lay in bed, letting the words speak what I couldn't.

It looked like journaling, not to make sense of everything, but just to get it out.

It looked like giving thanks for the smallest things: a good conversation, a few hours without pain, a moment of clarity.

It looked like not pushing away support when it came, even if all I could say was "thank you."

It looked like letting people love me, letting God hold me, and letting myself rest in the mystery of what I didn't yet understand.

Faith wasn't something I finally got right. It was something I returned to whenever I forgot that I didn't have to hold everything alone.

One night, I had been violently ill for hours, curled up on the bathroom floor, pouring out every ounce of strength I had left. I remember gripping the sides of the toilet after another wretched session—my eyes were heavy, my body was trembling, and my heart was numb. I had nothing left to give.

I wasn't praying with words anymore, just breath.

I didn't know if I could live like this. But I also knew I couldn't quit.

Somewhere between the shaking and the silence, I found myself leaning against the wall, eyes closed. And when I opened them again, the room wasn't dark anymore.

The sun was rising.

Light began pouring through the edges of the window. A new day had arrived.

And in that moment, I realized: *There is a tomorrow.*

It wasn't the perfect one I had been chasing or the one I was trying to control. It was the one that still came, despite it all.

That sunrise didn't fix me, but it reminded me of something I had forgotten in the night:

ROOTED, NOT RUSHED

Life was still moving, and somehow, so was I.

That night wasn't unusual. It had become part of the routine: another flare-up, another bout of sickness that took everything from me, another night praying to the porcelain gods for relief.

This was *my life now*. And somehow, even that had stopped shocking me.

But what happened after was different.

I had finally made it back to bed, still queasy and weak, but the edge had passed. I lay there in silence, somewhere between sleep and surrender, unsure if I should expect anything from the day ahead.

The light shifted.

It was pale at first, barely more than a suggestion. It softened the corners of the room. It didn't shout. It didn't rush. It just arrived.

That's what hope felt like for me that morning— not like fireworks, but like a quiet presence whispering, *"You made it to this moment. And that's enough."*

The room turned from gray to golden. And for some reason I still can't fully explain, I sat up, and I just watched.

That sunrise—after such a brutal, exhausting night—hit differently. A whisper in my spirit that said, *"This is life. It's hard. It hurts. And it's still worth it."*

I think we're taught to equate blessings with ease, but I've learned that life's truest blessings show up in the middle of the mess.

Beauty isn't in things being easy, but in seeing your strength clearly, *even when things are not.*

Not everything feels good.

Not everything goes right.

But *you're still here.*

You're still breathing.

You're still believing in something more.

And that's where hope lives—not in the perfect days, but in the courage to find light after the darkest ones.

INSIGHTS TO CONSIDER:

1. Faith in the Midst of Uncertainty

Faith isn't about having all the answers; it's about having the courage to move forward without them. It's a decision to trust even when clarity is absent.[1]

✧ Reflect: What areas of my life require me to step forward in faith, even when I don't see the entire path?

2. Embracing Surrender as Empowerment

Surrender isn't about giving up; it's about letting go of the need to control every detail of life. It's about releasing your attachment to specific outcomes and trusting that what's meant for you will unfold as it should.[2]

✧ Reflect: How do I feel about surrendering control? What would it look like if I let go of trying to force outcomes and allowed life to unfold more naturally?

3. Trusting Yourself in the Absence of Certainty

Trusting yourself means accepting that you have the ability to handle whatever comes your way, even when you can't predict the outcome. Faith in yourself doesn't require certainty; it's about trusting your resilience and resourcefulness.[3]

✧ Reflect: Where in my life do I need to trust my ability to handle uncertainty? What actions can I take today to build more trust in myself?

4. The Power of Being Present in the Now

When life feels uncertain, it's easy to get caught up in worries about the future. However, the key to finding peace is to ground yourself in the present moment. The future will unfold as it will, but you can control how you show up today.[4]

✧ Reflect: How often do I find myself anxious about the future? How can I practice staying present and engaged in the moment?

5. Clarity Often Follows Commitment

It's easy to feel paralyzed when you don't have all the information. But clarity often comes after you take the first step. Trust the process of becoming, and know that the path will reveal itself as you continue to move forward.[5]

✧ Reflect: What step can I take today, even a small one, that moves me forward, even if I'm not yet clear on the outcome?

PAUSE AND REFLECT:

Faith doesn't mean life gets easier.
It means we keep showing up, even when it's hard.

    1. What parts of my life have become "routine" pain, so familiar that I've stopped acknowledging how hard it is?

    Where have I been surviving in silence?

    2. What's one moment—however small—when I felt something shift in me?

    A breath, a realization, a sunrise. What did it remind me of?

    3. Have I been waiting for life to feel good before I believe it's beautiful?

    What would it look like to honor the beauty in the middle of the mess?

    4. In what ways has my faith grown quieter, but deeper?

    How do I now experience trust, surrender, or spiritual strength differently than I used to?

    5. What would it mean to see hope not as the absence of hardship, but as the choice to rise *with* it?

    Where in my life am I being invited to rise again?

The blessing isn't that it's easy.
The blessing is that you're still here—breathing, believing, becoming.
That's faith.

Chapter 12
The Truth You Can Trust

*"You've been criticizing yourself for years, and it hasn't worked.
Try approving of yourself and see what happens."*
—Louise Hay

No one talks about how hard it is to trust yourself again after life breaks you.

Your body has betrayed you.

Your voice has been silenced.

Your instincts have been ignored or mocked—sometimes by others, sometimes by you.

After years of people-pleasing, shape-shifting, and surviving, self-trust becomes a muscle you don't even realize you've let atrophy. Especially for high performers, self-trust becomes a complex issue. We're taught to excel, to anticipate needs, to lead from logic.

And slowly, without realizing it, we lose connection with the inner voice that once whispered clearly: *This is right. This is enough. This is me.* We're trained to keep moving, keep fixing, and keep winning. And the idea of stopping to check in with ourselves feels inefficient, or worse, indulgent.

But the truth is, no amount of achievement can compensate for a life lived out of alignment.

If we don't learn to trust our voice, we'll always be performing instead of living.

I didn't realize how deep the fracture had gone.

I could encourage everyone else with love, patience, and grace. But when it came to me,

I questioned everything.

Am I being too much?

Am I exaggerating this pain?

Am I the reason this is happening?

I didn't trust myself to rest.

I didn't trust myself to speak without overexplaining.

I didn't trust myself to know what I needed, because I had spent years tuning out my signals to accommodate the world.

It wasn't just my body that needed healing. It was my relationship with *myself.*

Every time I ignored that inner knowing, something else inside me grew quieter. Self-trust erodes slowly, until one day, you're second-guessing things you used to know without a doubt.

The answer isn't to get louder. It's to get still enough to hear again.

There were moments I sat in medical appointments and minimized my symptoms because I was afraid of being dismissed. There were days I felt emotionally flooded, but still tried to function like everything was fine. There were choices I made that honored everyone else, but not *me.*

And what I eventually realized was this: You can't rebuild your life without rebuilding trust in yourself first.

Your body *remembers* when you didn't listen.

Your heart remembers when you overrode your truth to avoid rocking the boat.

Your nervous system remembers when survival meant shrinking.

But self-trust isn't a sudden lightning bolt of confidence. It's built with quiet choices, in honoring your no, in breathing before reacting, and in leaving the room, the call, or the commitment when your body tells you it's too much.

You must listen more closely to the part of you that *knows*.

But we've always known. The challenge is giving ourselves permission to believe it.

As I rebuilt trust with myself, everything around me began to shift.

My relationships changed.

My leadership changed.

Even the way I showed up in my own home felt different.

I started paying attention to what I needed before I hit my breaking point. I let go of the pressure to prove myself at work, even if it meant people misunderstood me. I stopped saying yes out of fear of being left out or replaced. I started honoring my limitations *without first explaining them to everyone else.*

And the truth is, not everyone understood. Some relationships faded.

Some people made comments. But I no longer sacrificed my peace for their comfort.

And I didn't do it alone.

I had to create rituals that reminded me I was safe to be with myself again.

Over these past few years, especially since my health crash in 2020, self-trust has started to look like this:

Morning intention, not reaction: I stopped waking up and rushing into the noise of the world: no social media, no immediate emails, no chaos. Instead, I began my mornings rebuilding healthy habits that would carry me through the day—*habits that aligned with the woman I was becoming:* gratitude, gentle stretching, taking my vitamins, peptides, and medicines; meditating, praying, affirming, and protecting my peace before anything else was allowed in. I wasn't reacting to life anymore—I was showing up for it on purpose.

Using my time to support my values: I began living by my calendar and timers. These tools helped me stay consistent, establish a rhythm, and conserve my energy. It reminded me that discipline is an act of self-trust, not restriction, but *respect* for my time and well-being.

Healing my relationship with food: One of the most challenging aspects has been learning how to nourish a body that doesn't always respond well to being fed. Food sustains, but it has also triggered flare-ups and pain. So, I started building an environment of trust. I reminded myself to eat when my body didn't intuitively know how.

Resting without guilt: I don't just rest when I *hit the wall* anymore. I rest when my body whispers, not just when it screams, even when it feels inconvenient or when the guilt creeps in. Resting is not weakness. It's wisdom.

Small steps, big trust: There were days I couldn't even walk to the front door. Then one day, I made it to the end of the driveway, then a few steps beyond. Now, I find joy in gardening and being outside, within limits, with a sense of balance. It's not about "doing it all." It's about doing what *honors* the energy I have, and letting that be enough.

Saying no, staying flexible, and still trying: Some days I plan, and the day changes. Some days I cancel, and that's okay. The difference is I don't abandon myself in the process. I listen. I adjust. I try again.

These habits didn't come easily.

Even when I started with the best intentions— quiet morning, gratitude, and gentle movement—the moment my eyes opened, life pulled me in a dozen directions.

A message here. A deadline there. Someone else's needs. Someone else's expectations.

I didn't just need new habits.

I needed a new *foundation*.

I needed to wake up and say, *Today is built around what I need, not just what others expect.*

And that meant more than routines. It meant reimagining my relationships. I started walking into new rooms with the mindset of someone who had moved to a brand-new town.

I reintroduced myself, not to others, but *to me.*

I stopped expecting my old environments to understand the new version of who I was becoming.

Instead, I let those environments show me who I needed to be and where I needed to let go.

Self-trust taught me how to stop controlling the room and start listening to how the room made me feel.

I stopped proving.

I started *observing.*

I wasn't going to abandon *her* again: the little girl inside me who used to hide to stay safe, who learned early that her needs came second, who got so used to surviving that she stopped asking for what she needed.

This time, I listened.

Not to the outside noise.

Not to the voice of expectation or performance.

But to her.

I started asking myself: *What would feel safe right now?*

What does my body need to feel cared for?

What would the little girl in me want me to choose today?

The more I leaned into trust, the more I noticed something surprising: I was smiling and laughing more. I was feeling things with less fear of losing control. Trust made space for joy—the kind that's rooted, present, and real.

INSIGHTS TO CONSIDER:

1. Trust Begins with Self-Awareness

Trusting yourself requires awareness of your needs, your emotions, and your boundaries. It's not about being perfect; it's about being in tune with who you are and what you truly need at each moment.[1]

✧ Reflect: How aware am I of my needs and feelings? What would it look like to trust myself more fully by listening to my internal cues?

2. Rebuilding Trust Takes Patience

Trust isn't something that can be rebuilt overnight. It's a process that takes time, small actions, and compassion toward yourself when things don't go as planned. Be patient with the rebuilding process.[2]

✧ Reflect: Where do I need to be more patient with myself in the process of rebuilding trust? How can I make small, intentional actions to reinforce confidence in myself today?

3. The Power of Boundaries in Trust

One of the most important ways to rebuild trust with yourself is by setting and respecting boundaries. Boundaries are a form of self-respect and the foundation of self-trust.[3]

✧ Reflect: How have boundaries helped me in the past to build trust with myself and others? What boundaries can I set today that will reinforce my self-trust?

4. Trust Is a Practice, Not a Destination

We often think of trust as something that, once achieved, stays with us. However, trust is a practice—a continuous, active process that requires nurturing and attention. It doesn't mean perfection; it means returning to your center, time and time again.[4]

✧ Reflect: Where do I need to be more consistent in practicing trust with myself? What practices or rituals can I create to nurture self-trust every day?

5. Trust Yourself Enough to Let Go

Letting go of old stories, people-pleasing, and past trauma is essential to rebuilding trust with yourself. It's about recognizing that you are worthy of making decisions that prioritize your well-being.[5]

✧ Reflect: What old stories or people do I need to let go of in order to trust myself more fully? How can I begin to release them without guilt?

PAUSE AND REFLECT:

Self-trust is the quiet decision to stop abandoning yourself.
And to start choosing from a place of alignment, not fear.

1. Where in my life have I been over-functioning or over-performing to feel safe or worthy?

And how is that keeping me disconnected from myself?

2. What are the smallest signs that I've been ignoring from my body or inner voice?

Hunger, exhaustion, discomfort, intuition—what's been whispering?

3. What habits help me feel grounded, even if the rest of my day doesn't go as planned?

Where could I offer myself more structure, not for control, but for care?

4. What environments make me shrink, and which ones help me rise?

Where do I feel safe to be the truest version of me?

5. What would it look like to make decisions with my inner child in mind?

What does she need to feel seen, supported, and protected today?

Self-trust isn't a destination.
It's a relationship.
And the more you listen, the more you'll know exactly how to take care of yourself.

Chapter 13
Joy as a Form of Resistance

"To feel joy is not to betray the pain.
It is to honor the truth that you are still alive."
—Nayyirah Waheed

Joy used to feel like a reward—something I had to earn after everything else was done, and something I needed permission for.

When life became heavy, the pressure stacked high, and grief and pain and uncertainty took center stage, joy started to feel optional. It was something I didn't have time for.

But joy is not the absence of pain.

It's not naïve.

It's not irresponsible.

It's not a bypassing of reality.

Joy is an act of resistance, especially when the world tells you to hustle harder, numb faster, prove more.

Your past taught you that rest was laziness, that laughter was unsafe, that tenderness had to be earned.

Joy says: *I'm still here.*

It wasn't easy for me to get here because, for so long, I was in survival mode. I was doing what high achievers do best: pushing through, leading with performance, and chasing the gold stars of being needed.

But somewhere along the way, I realized: *What's the point of surviving if you forget how to live?*

I had to redefine what joy even meant for me: not the big vacations or the perfect days, but the tiny glimmers. I found joy in the first sip of coffee when it's quiet, the sun warming my face on the front porch, a text from someone who "just gets it," and the calm after the storm of a hard conversation where I finally spoke my truth.

Those moments saved me. I began looking for them, noticing them, and naming them.

Because when you live through something hard, your body learns to scan for danger. Your mind learns to prepare for worst-case scenarios. Your nervous system becomes a pro at anticipating the next hit.

Joy interrupts that pattern.

Joy is what retrains the mind to look for life instead of threat.

Joy is a rebellion against the belief that your worth is in your output.

Joy is the evidence that you're still here, and that something in you still wants to feel light.

At first, it felt awkward to laugh after so much pain, to dance in the kitchen when my body still ached, to say yes to something fun even when not everything was figured out yet.

But joy isn't waiting for the conditions to be perfect. Joy meets you where you are.

There were days I still couldn't do much. I didn't get dressed. I didn't leave the house. I didn't respond to messages. But even on those days, I could light a candle. I could open a window. I could sit in the quiet and whisper to myself, "This moment matters, too."

I began to notice how joy shifted things, not just for me, but for everyone around me. When I laughed more, my team relaxed more. When I paused to appreciate instead of only pushing, my leadership became more human. When I let joy in, I gave others permission to do the same.

This is what I mean by joy as resistance. It resists the idea that we must earn rest and that we need to be fully healed to enjoy our lives.

No. We need joy to heal. We need beauty to breathe. We need to feel something good, not as a distraction, but as a declaration: *I am still here.*

And if I'm here, I might as well live like it.

INSIGHTS TO CONSIDER:

It's not the end of the road when life feels tough—it's the moment you've gathered enough strength to press forward differently.

Just as a seed needs time and the right conditions to sprout and grow, your resilience needs space to expand. This isn't the final version of yourself; it's a new chapter, where you become who you've been meant to be, but with everything you've learned along the way. Life is full of cycles, and your story is ongoing. As you reflect on your journey, remember: Resilience is not about coming out unscathed, but about growing, adapting, and evolving despite the challenges.

It's about not letting the difficulties of life close you off to the possibilities ahead.

BEFORE YOU TURN THE PAGE...

This chapter was my story.

Now, I invite you to look at your own.

You don't have to wait for the hard season to end before you feel joy.

Joy is allowed to walk with your grief.

To visit you in your ordinary days.

To anchor you when everything feels unsteady.

What if joy isn't the result of healing, but part of the reason you keep healing?

PAUSE AND REFLECT:

Joy isn't a destination. It's a way of remembering who you are.

1. What does joy look like for me right now—not past me, not ideal me, but this version of me?

Allow yourself to define it differently than before. Let it be simple and real for the person you are today.

2. Where have I been waiting for life to get better before I let myself feel good again?

What would happen if I gave myself permission to feel joy in the middle of the mess?

3. What are the small "glimmers" that help my nervous system exhale?

List moments that bring calm, warmth, or a soft smile. These are your lifelines. What simple things in life bring you peace?

4. Where in my life am I still living like I have to earn joy, rest, or celebration?

Who taught me that, and is that belief still serving me? How can I begin to let go of the idea that I have to earn joy?

5. When was the last time I did something fun, without a reason, goal, or audience?

Let yourself play, explore, or enjoy just because you're alive. What would it feel like to reconnect with joy in its purest form?

6. What joy have I overlooked because I was focused on the "big picture"?

What's already present in my life right now that deserves more of my attention? How can I appreciate the little moments more fully?

7. How might joy be a form of resilience for me—not an escape, but a way back to myself?

Look for where joy has kept you grounded, even when life didn't make sense. How has joy been a form of resistance against hardship for you?

8. What would it look like to practice joy as a rhythm, not just an emotion?

How can I intentionally make space for what lights me up, even in small ways? What habits or rhythms could I create to invite more joy into my daily life?

You don't need permission to feel good.
You don't have to wait for the hard season to end.
Joy can live here, too, right in the middle of the mess.
And choosing it isn't weakness; it's resistance.

Chapter 14
The Work After the Work

"The true test of a man's character is what he does
when no one is watching."
—John Wooden

The work after the work isn't flashy.

It doesn't get you applause.

It doesn't come with a dramatic ending or a before-and-after photo.

It's quiet, repetitive, and sometimes boring, but it's sacred.

It's the part that proves to you that the growth wasn't a fluke, where you show up differently when no one's asking you to.

I had already survived the collapse. I had surrendered, softened, and realigned. I had rewritten my definition of success. But now I had to live it, even in the moments when it would have been easier to go back to the hustle, when the world tried to hand me my old identity again.

I had to protect this version of me. This challenged me in new ways. It's easy to make changes when the world is crashing down around you, but it's much harder to keep choosing differently when life starts to look normal again, when no one's watching.

~

That's when the old habits try to sneak back in, under the guise of being "efficient," or "productive," or "what's expected."

That's when the real work shows up. It's not dramatic. It's a quiet decision in the middle of a Tuesday afternoon to take a break, even though your calendar says keep going. It's recognizing when your "go mode" isn't inspiration but fear. It's catching yourself before you spiral. That's the work most people never see. But it's the work that shapes everything.

Healing changes your standards and shifts what you're willing to tolerate. For me, those new standards manifested in conversations I used to avoid, in the way I handled being interrupted, and in how I handled myself when no one else followed through.

I stopped tolerating disrespect.

I stopped tolerating urgency that didn't align with my peace.

I stopped tolerating the voice in my head that said, *You're behind.*

My standards didn't make me harder to please.

They made me easier to trust.

That kind of clarity takes work to maintain.

Some days, that work looked like using my calendar as a boundary I could trust. Other days, it looked like turning off my phone before bed, even when my mind was restless. Sometimes, it looked like saying no to people I used to say yes to automatically, even if it made me feel guilty.

More often than not, the work was invisible.

The work after the work is integration. It's where I learned to live from the healed place, not just visit it.

Even after all the healing, I still have to re-become myself again and again. There are still hard days. There are still flare-ups. There are still temptations to default to the old rhythm.

But now, I recognize the signals faster.

I recover quicker.

I forgive myself more easily.

I return to myself with less shame and more compassion.

That's the work: honoring the fact that you're still here, still listening, and still showing up.

INSIGHTS TO CONSIDER:

I. Real Change Happens in the Repetition

"Real change happens not when we decide to become someone different, but when we start showing up as that person consistently-even when it's inconvenient."

The brain creates and reinforces neural pathways based on repetition. According to neuroscientist Dr. Lisa Feldman Barrett, your brain doesn't wait passively for instructions; it predicts. That means how you live today becomes the blueprint for tomorrow. The habits you choose, the boundaries you uphold, the rest you prioritize—these aren't small maintenance tasks. They're how your brain rewires itself to support who you're becoming.[1]

✧ Reflect:

- Where are you waiting to feel "ready" instead of committing to the rhythm?
- What are the micro-decisions you make each day that reinforce who you want to be?

2. Identity-Based Habits Anchor Your Growth

"True behavior change is identity change. You're not just building new routines—you're building a new relationship with yourself."

Author and behavioral expert James Clear emphasizes that lasting transformation is anchored in *who you believe you are.* You're not just someone who goes to bed earlier or blocks time for self-care. You become someone who prioritizes rest, who honors alignment, who lives intentionally. Identity-based habits create the deepest roots.[2]

✧ Reflect:

- When I look at my current routines, do they reflect the identity I'm living from, the one I'm growing into?
- What small habit can I commit to as a vote for the version of me I'm protecting now?

3. Post-Crisis Growth Is a Process

"Growth doesn't end when the crisis does. In fact, that's often when it begins."

Psychologists Richard Tedeschi and Lawrence Calhoun coined the term *Post-Traumatic Growth* to describe the positive psychological changes that emerge in the wake of adversity. But growth isn't automatic; it requires reflection, deliberate effort, and a safe environment to thrive. The "after" is where your healing deepens and your resilience matures.[3]

✧ Reflect:

- Am I giving myself space to continue growing, or have I expected myself to be "done"?
- What internal signs show me that I'm still integrating the lessons I've learned?

PAUSE AND REFLECT:

You've already done the hard part.
Now comes the honest part: the becoming that lasts.

1. What parts of my healing have I only visited, but not yet fully integrated?

Where am I still tempted to go back to what's familiar, even if it no longer fits?

2. What does "maintenance" look like for the life I want?

What boundaries, rhythms, or check-ins help me stay aligned, not just once, but over time?

3. What does it mean to me to "live" the healing, not just talk about it?

How does that show up in my work, relationships, or daily routines?

4. What version of myself am I protecting now?

Not the one I used to be, not the one I feel pressured to become, but the one I'm becoming today. What does this version of me need most?

5. **What internal signals tell me I'm starting to slip into old patterns?**

How can I notice them sooner and respond with care instead of criticism?

6. **What simple rituals or choices help me return to myself without shame?**

List one or two daily actions that serve as anchors to your truth, even on hard days.

7. **Where do I still feel like I have something to prove?**

What would it mean to let that go and trust that the work I've done is already enough?

8. **What does it mean to re-become myself, over and over again, without guilt or performance?**

How can I welcome my evolution as something beautiful, even if it's still in process?

The work after the work isn't about being perfect.
It's about choosing your peace again and again, even when no one else sees you doing it.

Chapter 15
This Is Not the End

"You were never meant to shrink to fit.
You were meant to rise to full height."
—Morgan Harper Nichols

I didn't write this book because I'm healed. I didn't write it because I have a cure. I wrote it because even in the middle of a life I didn't choose, I found something worth holding onto: not the milestones, not the applause, but the small, sacred truths that rose to the surface when everything else fell away.

I found the feeling of breath coming back after a long night, the warmth of light on my face that reminds me the world is still spinning, the quiet strength that whispers, *Not yet. Don't give up.*

That's what I held onto. And that's what I want to pass on to you.

I found purpose in the process.

There was a time when I believed that everything had to be fixed to be worthy of being shared. Stories only had value once they had a redemptive arc. But life rarely wraps itself up with a bow. And wholeness isn't found in the resolution; it's found in the willingness to stay present through the unraveling.

I had to unlearn the myth that becoming meant "arriving," and instead, I had to embrace that becoming is a rhythm. It's not a title you earn. It's a choice you keep making.

I don't have a finish line to offer you, but I do know this:

You don't need a cure to be whole.

You don't need a title to be worthy.

You don't need approval to be seen.

You need permission to live as you are.

And maybe, you don't need to wait for life to look how you imagined it before you begin again.

Sometimes, we become the most grounded version of ourselves in the rubble.

Let me say this clearly: You are not here to apologize for your softness, or your slowness, or your strength that doesn't look like everyone else's.

Sometimes becoming looks like nothing special. It looks like sitting in your car in silence before walking into a room. It looks like standing at your kitchen sink, hands in warm water, wondering if this is all there is—and then remembering, *Yes, this matters*. It looks like replying to a message you've been avoiding, with honesty this time. It's not dramatic. It's not glamorous. But it is courageous. And it counts.

You are allowed to carry both grit and grief.

You are allowed to be the strong one and still need to rest.

You are allowed to rise in ways that don't make sense to anyone else, because they're not walking your path.

And this moment, this chapter, this breath is not your ending.

It's a return.

A remembering.

A reclaiming of the parts of you that survival made you forget.

You don't have to have all the answers to keep moving.

You don't have to feel brave to be brave.

You just have to keep going.

And maybe you won't walk away with everything fixed, but perhaps that's not the point.

Maybe the gift is knowing you're still here, and that's enough to begin again.

Becoming doesn't mean you've arrived. It means you've decided to keep choosing growth even when it's slow, even when it's hard, and no one sees the effort but you. It means you've stopped measuring yourself by what you produce and started measuring yourself by how present you're willing to be. It means you are learning to belong to yourself before you ever ask the world to understand you.

This is not the end. It is the next breath.

You are not behind.

You are not broken.

You are not too late.

You are becoming.

And if you ever forget, come back here. This isn't a one-time read. It's a place to return to, a page to hold in your hands when the world feels too loud again, and a reminder that resilience isn't something you earn once; it's something you keep choosing.

And I'll be right here with you every time you do.

INSIGHTS TO CONSIDER:

1. Resilience Is a Rhythm, Not a Result

"Resilience is built in the small, daily decisions to stay open, to stay soft, to stay in it-even when it would be easier to shut down."

Resilience isn't a single heroic act but a continual return. Research from the American Psychological Association defines resilience not as avoiding stress, but as adapting and growing through it. That growth often happens in cycles—moments of stretching, contracting, re-rooting, and rising again.[1]

✧ Reflect:

- How have I mistaken resilience for perfection or always being strong?
- In what ways am I already resilient, even if no one else sees it?

2. Insight to Consider: The Brain Learns Through Repatterning

"Every time you choose to respond differently, even just once, you're carving a new neural path."

Neuroplasticity tells us the brain is capable of change throughout life. This means that every gentle choice, every pause before reacting, and every moment you show up in new alignment becomes part of how your mind and body wire for stability and growth. It's not about erasing the old; it's about reinforcing the new.[2]

✧ Reflect:

- Where am I already choosing differently?
- What repeated response or belief am I ready to replace, one small shift at a time?

3. Insight to Consider: Becoming Is a Lifelong Process

"Healing doesn't mean you arrive at wholeness; it means you remember it's been with you all along."
Carl Jung once wrote, *"I am not what happened to me, I am what I choose to become."* Healing doesn't always make the pain disappear, but it restores your agency. Becoming is an invitation to meet yourself—again and again—with clarity, care, and curiosity.[3]
✧ Reflect:

- How do I define "healed?" Is that definition helping or hindering my growth?
- What part of me am I rediscovering, not creating from scratch, but remembering?

Epilogue
A Note From Me to You

If you've made it this far, I want to tell you something:

Thank you.

Thank you for walking this road with me.

For staying.

For listening.

For making space, not just for my story, but for your own.

Writing this book wasn't easy. It asked me to revisit pain, grief, silence, shame, and transformation. But more than anything, it asked me to tell the truth, and in doing so, I found something I didn't expect: a deeper connection to people like you.

People who know what it means to fall and rise.

People who have been silenced but never stopped listening for the sound of their voice.

People who carry so much and still find the courage to try again.

I don't know where your journey will take you next. I don't know what you're holding.

But I know this:

You don't have to do it perfectly.

You don't have to have it all figured out.

You just have to keep choosing yourself, softly, daily, and rooted without an apology.

The world doesn't need a flawless version of you. It needs the real one, the becoming one, the one who keeps showing up.

I hope this book was more than a read. I hope it was a reflection and a reclaiming.

And if no one else tells you today:

I'm proud of you.

I see you.

Keep going.

Acknowledgments

Before I thank anyone else, I need to start here—with God, and with her: the little girl, in me, who hid in closets, the one who learned silence before she ever learned safety, the one who felt unseen, unheard, and unsure she'd ever be whole.

She is the beginning of this book.

She is the heartbeat of every word on these pages.

She is who I look for in the mirror when I need to remember who I really am.

And to God: Thank You for never letting go of me. You saw her. You stayed with her. You gave her the strength to survive, You gave me the grace to find her roots again, and to finally become the woman You always intended for me to be. You heard every cry in the dark when no one else did. You stayed through the fear, through the fight, through the parts of my story I didn't think I'd make it through. You are the reason I'm still here. All glory, all healing, all purpose that came from this book belongs first to You.

There were days I didn't think I'd survive, or maybe I didn't want to. There were moments I couldn't find my voice, see my future, show my strength, or even summon the will to keep going.

But I did.

By grace.

By grit.

By the quiet mercy that met me in the middle of the mess and said, *Not yet; there's more for you.*

This book was never about the perfect ending.

It's about *resilience in motion.*

And I didn't get here alone.

To my husband: You were my strength when I had none. Thank you for standing in the fire with me, for advocating when I couldn't speak, and for showing me the art of real love. You've never wavered, even when the storms were relentless. You held my hand through the worst of it and reminded me, over and over, that I was never alone. Your quiet strength, your loyalty, and your love have shaped this journey in ways no words can fully capture.

To my children: You are my why. You are the reason I chose to keep fighting, even when everything in me was tired. You gave me purpose in my pain, light in my darkest days, and the deepest joy I've ever known. Every day I choose to rise is because of you. I hope this book shows you what resilience looks like—and reminds you that you, too, can keep going through whatever becomes.

To my parents: Thank you for doing the best you could with what you had. Thank you for your love, your presence, and your place in my story. Through your sacrifices, I learned strength. Through your lessons, I found growth. Thank you for being part of the roots that ground me.

To those who challenged me: Yes, even you. To the ones who doubted me, dismissed me, or tried to quiet my voice, thank you. Your resistance became the mirror I needed to see myself more clearly. You pushed me to find my boundaries, to speak louder, and to rise higher than I thought I could. For that, I'm grateful.

To the reader holding this book: Thank you for showing up. Thank you for making space for me, and more importantly, for yourself. I hope something in these pages reminded you that you're not alone. That you're allowed to fall and rise. That resilience is already living inside you.

And that your story, just like mine, is still unfolding.

We are all still becoming.

And I'm honored to walk a part of your journey with you.

With love and deep gratitude,
Mairin

Becoming: Companion Workbook

A guided space to reflect, reimagine, and return to yourself.

This section is not about doing more. It's about becoming more present.

You've just walked through a journey of truth-telling, resilience, and reclamation. Now, I invite you to pause—not to fix anything, but to feel what's still stirring in you.

The following few pages are here to help you:

- Anchor what resonated most.
- Hear your voice more clearly.
- Make space for the wisdom you already hold.

You don't have to fill out every line. You don't have to have the "right" answers. This is your space. Come back to it anytime you feel lost, unsure, or ready to remember who you are.

Let's begin.

Chapter 1: What I Thought Was Strength

The foundation: Early patterns, survival instincts, and the roots of resilience

This space is for you. There's no pressure to write the "right" thing, just your truth as it stands today. Let your answers be honest, unfinished, and real. Your growth deserves to be seen.

Reflection Prompt:

1. What survival strategies did I learn early on that once kept me safe, but now limit me?
2. Where in my life have I confused strength with silence?
3. What old beliefs am I ready to release so I can breathe more fully?

Journal Space: *Write to the younger version of yourself. The one who learned to carry too much. What does she/he deserve to know now?*

_____

_____

_____

_____

_____

_____

_____

_____

Chapter 2: The Becoming Begins

The unraveling: Identity, pressure, performance—and a quiet shift toward change

This space is for you. There's no pressure to write the "right" thing, just your truth as it stands today. Let your answers be honest, unfinished, and real. Your growth deserves to be seen.

Reflection Prompt:

1. In what ways have I tied my worth to what I can produce or achieve?
2. When have I ignored my own needs in order to maintain an image of being "fine?"
3. What did I learn about identity from my work or accomplishments that I now want to unlearn?
4. Where in my life do I crave release from expectations, roles, or pressure to perform?
5. What does it look like to become, not by doing more, but by being more myself?

Journal Space: *Write a letter to the version of you who was always "on." The one who held it all together, even when it was costing you something. What do they need to hear from you now?*

_____

_____

_____

_____

_____

_____

_____

_____

_____

_____

_____

_____

_____

_____

_____

_____

_____

_____

_____

_____

_____

_____

Chapter 3: Living On Purpose

Boundaries, realignment, and redefining what matters most

This space is for you. There's no pressure to write the "right" thing, just your truth as it stands today. Let your answers be honest, unfinished, and real. Your growth deserves to be seen.

Reflection Prompt:

1. What beliefs have I outgrown that I'm still living by?
2. Where am I saying yes out of habit, fear, or guilt instead of alignment?
3. Who in my life supports the version of me that is becoming, not the one I've outgrown?
4. What boundary could I set right now that would bring me peace, not guilt?
5. How do I want to feel in my daily life, and what would need to change to support that feeling?

Journal Space: *Write a vision for what it means to live on purpose in this next season of your life. What rhythms, values, and boundaries support the version of you who is thriving, not just surviving?*

_____

_____

_____

_____

_____

_____

_____

_____

_____

_____

_____

_____

_____

_____

_____

_____

_____

_____

_____

_____

_____

_____

_____

Chapter 4: Soft Doesn't Mean Small

Reclaiming softness, shifting leadership, and finding strength in intention

This space is for you. There's no pressure to write the "right" thing, just your truth as it stands today. Let your answers be honest, unfinished, and real. Your growth deserves to be seen.

Reflection Prompt:

1. What have I been taught about strength, and is that definition still true for me?
2. Where in my life have I quieted my voice to keep the peace or appear "together?"
3. What would it feel like to stop performing and start showing up as my whole self in work, in relationships, in leadership?
4. Where could I lead, speak, or live from love instead of fear?
5. What might soften in me if I stopped trying to be so "strong" all the time?

Journal Space: *Write to the version of you that thought softness made you less capable.*

What would you want them to know about what strength really looks like now?

_____

_____

_____

_____

_____

_____

Chapter 5: The In-Between Is Still Sacred

Redefining progress, honoring grief, and trusting the slow work of becoming

This space is for you. There's no pressure to write the "right" thing, just your truth as it stands today. Let your answers be honest, unfinished, and real. Your growth deserves to be seen.

Reflection Prompt:

1. What have I lost or let go of that still carries grief?
2. Where in my life have I mistaken the in-between for failure instead of transformation?
3. What is quietly growing within me, even if I haven't seen the full bloom yet?
4. What small habit, boundary, or belief could support the life I want to build moving forward?
5. Who am I becoming, even if no one else sees it yet?

Journal Space: *Write to the version of yourself standing in the in-between—the one navigating change, holding grief, and still showing up. What do they need to hear from you right now?*

_____

_____

_____

_____

_____

_____

_____

_____

_____

_____

_____

_____

_____

_____

_____

_____

_____

_____

_____

_____

_____

_____

_____

Chapter 6: The Body Keeps the Wisdom

Listening to the body, honoring what it carries, and beginning again with compassion

This space is for you. There's no pressure to write the "right" thing, just your truth as it stands today. Let your answers be honest, unfinished, and real. Your growth deserves to be seen.

Reflection Prompt:

1. What physical signals have I been brushing off, minimizing, or powering through?
2. When does my body feel safe? Who or what helps create that environment?
3. How has my body been asking for care, and how have I responded?
4. What is one moment I now realize my body was trying to speak to me? What was it saying?
5. What would it look like to move through my days in partnership with my body, rather than in control of it?
6. What does my body need from me right now, and how can I offer it?

Journal Space: *Write a letter to your body. You might want to apologize.*

You might want to thank it. You might just want to sit beside it in truth.

Let it be what it needs to be.

_____

_____

_____

_____

_____

Chapter 7: The Grief No One Talks About

Honoring invisible losses, redefining resilience, and making space for what still aches

This space is for you. There's no pressure to write the "right" thing, just your truth as it stands today. Let your answers be honest, unfinished, and real. Your growth deserves to be seen.

Reflection Prompt:

1. What part of my story am I still grieving, even if it seems "small" to others?
2. What have I lost that no one else may have noticed?
3. Where have I shown up—tired, tender, unsure, but still present?
4. What would it look like to let myself grieve without rushing to feel "better?"
5. Where in my life has grief invited growth or shifted my view of strength?

Journal Space: *Write a few words for the version of yourself who lived through the loss.*

What did they need that they didn't receive? What can you offer that version of you now?

_____

_____

_____

_____

_____

_____

_____

_____

_____

_____

_____

_____

_____

_____

_____

_____

_____

_____

_____

_____

_____

_____

_____

Chapter 8: The Courage to Be Seen

Letting go of perfection, reclaiming your voice, and stepping into visibility

This space is for you. There's no pressure to write the "right" thing, just your truth as it stands today. Let your answers be honest, unfinished, and real. Your growth deserves to be seen.

Reflection Prompt:

1. Where have I been holding back my truth, out of fear of being misunderstood or dismissed?
2. What past experience taught me to silence myself, and am I still living by that rule now?
3. Who helps me feel fully seen, and what is it about their presence that invites my voice?
4. What have I carried, created, or accomplished in silence? What do I want to name now?
5. What would I say if I weren't trying to be polite, perfect, or palatable?

Journal Space: *Write a letter to your voice. The one that went quiet. The one you're learning to trust again. What would you say to that version of you that stayed hidden for too long?*

_____

_____

_____

_____

_____

_____

_____

_____

_____

_____

_____

_____

_____

_____

_____

_____

_____

_____

_____

_____

_____

_____

_____

_____

_____

Chapter 9: Success, Redefined

Letting go of comparison, reclaiming purpose, and measuring life on your own terms

This space is for you. There's no pressure to write the "right" thing, just your truth as it stands today. Let your answers be honest, unfinished, and real. Your growth deserves to be seen.

Reflection Prompt:

1. How have I defined success up until now, and whose version of success have I been chasing?
2. What would success look like if I let it be slower, softer, or more honest?
3. Where in my life am I still measuring worth by output or recognition?
4. What makes me feel most grounded, most present, most alive— and how can I honor that more often?
5. What does success feel like—not what does it look like?

Journal Space: *Write a declaration of your new definition of success. Be specific. Be bold.*

Let this be a moment where you choose what matters most— no more proving, just becoming.

_____

_____

_____

_____

_____

_____

Chapter 10: The Power of Saying No

Honoring capacity, protecting peace, and learning to love without overextending

This space is for you. There's no pressure to write the "right" thing, just your truth as it stands today. Let your answers be honest, unfinished, and real. Your growth deserves to be seen.

Reflection Prompt:

1. What have I been saying yes to that's no longer aligned with who I am or how I want to live?
2. Where have I ignored my limits out of fear of disappointing others or being misunderstood?
3. How does it feel when I say yes from obligation versus alignment?
4. Who in my life respects my boundaries, and who resists them? What does that reveal?
5. What boundary is my life asking me to set right now, and what freedom might come from honoring it?

Journal Space: *Write a "no" you've been holding back—one that would honor your peace, your energy, or your truth. Then, write a few new "yeses" you're ready to reclaim because you made that space.*

_____

_____

_____

_____

_____

_____

_____

Chapter 11: Faith in the Fog

Letting go of control, choosing trust, and finding light in the middle of the dark

This space is for you. There's no pressure to write the "right" thing, just your truth as it stands today. Let your answers be honest, unfinished, and real. Your growth deserves to be seen.

Reflection Prompt:

1. What parts of my life have become "routine" pain—so familiar that I've stopped acknowledging how hard it is?
2. When have I felt something shift, even subtly, in my perspective or spirit? What reminded me I was still here?
3. Have I been waiting for clarity before trusting the process? What would it look like to move with uncertainty instead of resisting it?
4. Where in my life have I been gripping too tightly for control? What might surrender look like there?
5. What would it mean to redefine faith, not as certainty, but as a quiet willingness to keep showing up?

Journal Space: *Write about a moment when life felt heavy, and something, however small, reminded you to keep going. It might be a sunrise, a word, a feeling. What did that moment give you?*

_____

_____

_____

_____

_____

_____

Chapter 12: The Truth You Can Trust

Rebuilding self-trust after survival, performance, and disconnection

This space is for you. There's no pressure to write the "right" thing, just your truth as it stands today. Let your answers be honest, unfinished, and real. Your growth deserves to be seen.

Reflection Prompt:

1. Where in my life have I been over-functioning or over-performing to feel safe or worthy?
2. What signs—physical, emotional, or spiritual—have I ignored that were trying to speak to me?
3. What would it look like to rebuild trust with myself, one small choice at a time?
4. What routines, relationships, or environments help me feel grounded, safe, and clear?
5. If I could speak directly to my younger self, what would I say to remind them they are safe to be who they are now?

Journal Space: *Write a letter to yourself from the version of you who fully trusts your voice.*

Let this future version speak encouragement, compassion, and strength into who you are today.

_____

_____

_____

_____

_____

Chapter 13: Joy as a Form of Resistance

Reclaiming beauty, presence, and light, even in the midst of hardship

This space is for you. There's no pressure to write the "right" thing, just your truth as it stands today. Let your answers be honest, unfinished, and real. Your growth deserves to be seen.

Reflection Prompt:

1. What moments of joy have I experienced recently, no matter how small?
2. How have I been taught (explicitly or subtly) that joy must be earned?
3. Where in my life am I still waiting for things to be "better" before allowing myself to feel joy?
4. What are the people, practices, or places that help me feel light and alive?
5. How might joy be a radical, healing choice for the season I'm in?

Journal Space: *Reflect on a moment when joy surprised you. Describe it fully—what you saw, felt, heard, or noticed. Then, explore how that moment can serve as a reminder of what's still possible.*

_____

_____

_____

_____

_____

_____

Chapter 14: The Work After the Work

Living the growth you fought for—quietly, consistently, and on purpose

This space is for you. There's no pressure to write the "right" thing, just your truth as it stands today. Let your answers be honest, unfinished, and real. Your growth deserves to be seen.

Reflection Prompt:

1. What parts of me are still learning to live in alignment with who I've become?
2. What habits, routines, or relationships support the life I say I want? Which ones quietly pull me backward?
3. Where am I still tempted to default to the old rhythm, even though I know better now?
4. What does "maintenance" look like for me emotionally, physically, and spiritually?
5. How do I know when I'm slipping into performance instead of presence?

Journal Space: *Write a letter to the version of yourself who first started this journey—the one just beginning to unravel or rebuild. Remind them what you know now about staying the course, even when the applause fades and the real work begins.*

_____

_____

_____

_____

_____

_____

_____

_____

_____

_____

_____

_____

_____

_____

_____

_____

_____

_____

_____

_____

_____

_____

_____

_____

_____

_____

Chapter 15: This Is Not the End

Resilience is not a moment; it's a rhythm. This is your invitation to keep choosing growth, even here.

This space is for you. There's no pressure to write the "right" thing, just your truth as it stands today. Let your answers be honest, unfinished, and real. Your growth deserves to be seen.

Reflection Prompt:

1. Where in my life do I still feel like I'm "waiting to arrive?"
2. What would change if I saw this season not as an end, but as a beginning?
3. What part of me is still learning how to belong to myself?
4. How do I want to define resilience for myself moving forward?
5. What would it look like to trust that I am not behind, but becoming?

Journal Space: *Write to your future self. Not the perfect version. Not the one who's "arrived." Just the next you—the one who is still becoming. Tell them what you hope they remember about this moment, this choice, this version of you.*

_____

_____

_____

_____

_____

_____

_____

_____

_____

_____

_____

_____

_____

_____

_____

_____

_____

_____

_____

_____

_____

_____

_____

Epilogue: A Note From Me to You

You don't have to have it all figured out. You just have to keep showing up. Becoming is not a finish line; it's your life unfolding.

This space is for you. There's no pressure to write the "right" thing, just your truth as it stands today. Let your answers be honest, unfinished, and real. Your growth deserves to be seen.

Reflection Prompt:

1. What have I discovered about myself through this process?
2. How have I redefined what healing, strength, and purpose mean to me?
3. Where do I still feel uncertain—and how can I show up with gentleness in that space?
4. What practices, truths, or reminders do I want to carry with me as I keep becoming?
5. If I forget everything else, what's one message from this book that I want to hold onto?

Journal Space: *Write a note to your current self. Celebrate who you are today—not just what you've overcome, but how you've continued to show up. This is your moment to honor your becoming.*

_____

_____

_____

_____

_____

_____

_____

_____

_____

_____

_____

_____

_____

_____

_____

_____

_____

_____

_____

_____

_____

_____

_____

_____

_____

Bonus Section: Dear Future Me

This space is yours, a letter to the version of you who's still becoming. Speak with honesty, kindness, and vision. This isn't about fixing; it's about remembering who you are, what you've survived, and where you still want to go.

Dear Future Me,

What I want you to remember is...

_____

_____

What I hope you never forget, even when it gets hard...

_____

_____

The strength you carry now comes from...

_____

_____

Here's what I dream for you:

_____

_____

Here's what I love about you, even on the days you don't see it:

_____

_____

And here's what I hope you always choose:

_____

_____

Keep going. You're becoming more than you know.

With love,

_____

Next Steps: Keep Becoming

This book may be coming to an end, but your journey is still unfolding. Becoming isn't a finish line; it's a rhythm, a relationship with yourself, and a daily invitation to show up, even when it's hard.

Here are a few ways you can keep the momentum going:

1. Revisit the pages that moved you.

Mark the chapters, prompts, or passages that stirred something in you. Let them become a compass for where you're headed next. Growth doesn't always come from new information—sometimes it's from deeper integration.

2. Create a personal check-in ritual.

Whether weekly or monthly, carve out intentional time to reflect:

- Where am I out of alignment?
- What feels like peace?
- What needs more attention or care? Small moments of honesty create significant shifts over time.

3. Choose one habit to nourish your present.

Pick one habit that supports the version of you you're becoming. It could be:

- A morning routine that begins with breath instead of busyness.
- Saying no once a week to something that drains you.
- Speaking your truth, one sentence more than you did last time.

4. Invite safe connection.

Healing happens in honest spaces. Find or create a community where you don't have to perform, fix, or filter. Whether it's one friend, a journal group, or a mentor, your story deserves a witness.

5. Anchor yourself with your "why."

Write it. Frame it. Tattoo it (if that's your thing). When life feels loud again, your *why* will bring you home.
Why are you choosing healing?
Why are you becoming?

6. Return to this book anytime.

These pages aren't going anywhere, and neither is your growth. Let this be a place you return to when you need courage, clarity, or a reminder that you're not alone.

You don't need a perfect plan. You just need presence.
One breath. One choice. One step at a time.
Keep rooted in your becoming. No need to rush. The world needs who you are.

There's nothing more beautiful than a person who chooses to rise each time they fall, becoming something greater in the process."
—Author Unknown

Notes

1. What I Thought Was Strength

1. Center on the Developing Child at Harvard University, *InBrief: The Impact of Early Adversity on Children's Development* (PDF, October 2024), https://developingchild.harvard.edu/wp-content/uploads/2024/10/inbrief-adversity-1.pdf.

2. The Becoming Begins

1. Jennifer Crocker and Connie T. Wolfe, "Contingencies of Self-Worth," *Psychological Review* 108, no. 3 (2001): 593–623.
2. Christina Maslach and Michael P. Leiter, *The Truth About Burnout: How Organizations Cause Personal Stress and What to Do About It* (San Francisco: Jossey-Bass, 1997).
3. Norman Doidge, *The Brain That Changes Itself: Stories of Personal Triumph from the Frontiers of Brain Science* (New York: Viking, 2007).

3. Living on Purpose

1. Bessel van der Kolk, *The Body Keeps the Score: Brain, Mind, and Body in the Healing of Trauma* (New York: Viking, 2014).
2. Robert M. Sapolsky, *Why Zebras Don't Get Ulcers* (New York: Henry Holt, 2004).
3. Martin E. P. Seligman, *Flourish: A Visionary New Understanding of Happiness and Well-Being* (New York: Free Press, 2011).

4. Soft Doesn't Mean Small

1. Stephen W. Porges, *The Polyvagal Theory: Neurophysiological Foundations of Emotions, Attachment, Communication, and Self-Regulation* (New York: W. W. Norton, 2011).
2. *Harvard Business Review*, "Emotional Intelligence and Leadership," July 2019.
3. Brené Brown, *Daring Greatly: How the Courage to Be Vulnerable Transforms the Way We Live, Love, Parent, and Lead* (New York: Gotham Books, 2012).

5. The In-Between Is Still Sacred

1. Richard Rohr, *Falling Upward: A Spirituality for the Two Halves of Life* (San Francisco: Jossey-Bass, 2011).
2. American Psychological Association, *Trauma and Post-Traumatic Growth* (Washington, DC: APA, 2022).
3. William Bridges, *Transitions: Making Sense of Life's Changes* (Reading, MA: Addison-Wesley, 1980).

6. The Body Keeps the Wisdom

1. Porges, *The Polyvagal Theory*, 2011.
2. van der Kolk, *The Body Keeps the Score*, 2014.
3. National Institute for the Clinical Application of Behavioral Medicine, *Building Internal Safety Through Everyday Habits* (2021).

7. The Grief No One Talks About

1. David Kessler, *Finding Meaning: The Sixth Stage of Grief* (New York: Scribner, 2019).
2. Sheryl Sandberg and Adam Grant, *Option B: Facing Adversity, Building Resilience, and Finding Joy* (New York: Knopf, 2017).
3. Elisabeth Kübler-Ross and David Kessler, *On Grief and Grieving: Finding the Meaning of Grief Through the Five Stages of Loss* (New York: Scribner, 2005).

8. The Courage to Be Seen

1. Brown, *Daring Greatly*, 2012.
2. Maya Angelou, *I Know Why the Caged Bird Sings* (New York: Random House, 1969).
3. Deepak Chopra, *The Seven Spiritual Laws of Success: A Practical Guide to the Fulfillment of Your Dreams* (San Rafael, CA: Amber-Allen Publishing, 1994).
4. Brené Brown, *Rising Strong: How the Ability to Reset Transforms the Way We Live, Love, Parent, and Lead* (New York: Spiegel & Grau, 2015).

9. Success, Redefined

1. Bessie Anderson Stanley, "Success," *Brown Book Magazine*, 1905.
2. Arianna Huffington, *Thrive: The Third Metric to Redefining Success and Creating a Life of Well-Being, Wisdom, and Wonder* (New York: Harmony Books, 2014).
3. Greg McKeown, *Essentialism: The Disciplined Pursuit of Less* (New York: Crown Business, 2014).
4. Carol S. Dweck, *Mindset: The New Psychology of Success* (New York: Random House, 2006).
5. Simon Sinek, *The Infinite Game* (New York: Portfolio, 2019).

10. The Power of Saying No

1. Henry Cloud and John Townsend, *Boundaries: When to Say Yes, How to Say No to Take Control of Your Life* (Grand Rapids, MI: Zondervan, 1992).
2. Lori Deschene, *Tiny Buddha: Simple Wisdom for Life's Hard Questions* (Berkeley, CA: Conari Press, 2011).
3. Brown, *Daring Greatly*, 2012.
4. McKeown, *Essentialism*, 2014.
5. Alexandra H. Solomon, *Loving Bravely: Twenty Lessons of Self-Discovery to Help You Get the Love You Want* (Oakland, CA: New Harbinger Publications, 2016).

Notes

11. Faith in the Fog

1. Neil L. Andersen, "Choose to Believe," *Latter-day Saint Insights*, 2015. https://latterday saintinsights.byu.edu/en/choose-to-believe/.
2. Eckhart Tolle, *The Power of Now: A Guide to Spiritual Enlightenment* (Novato, CA: New World Library, 1997).
3. Brown, *Daring Greatly*, 2012.
4. Jon Kabat-Zinn, *Wherever You Go, There You Are: Mindfulness Meditation in Everyday Life* (New York: Hyperion, 1994).
5. James Clear, *Atomic Habits: An Easy & Proven Way to Build Good Habits & Break Bad Ones* (New York: Avery, 2018).

12. The Truth You Can Trust

1. Tara Brach, *Radical Acceptance: Embracing Your Life With the Heart of a Buddha* (New York: Bantam Books, 2004).
2. Brené Brown, *The Gifts of Imperfection: Let Go of Who You Think You're Supposed to Be and Embrace Who You Are* (Center City, MN: Hazelden, 2010).
3. Cloud and Townsend, *Boundaries*, 1992.
4. Iyanla Vanzant, *In the Meantime: Finding Yourself and the Love You Want* (New York: Simon & Schuster, 1998).
5. Louise L. Hay, *You Can Heal Your Life* (Carlsbad, CA: Hay House, 1984).

14. The Work After the Work

1. Lisa Feldman Barrett, *How Emotions Are Made: The Secret Life of the Brain* (New York: Houghton Mifflin Harcourt, 2017).
2. Clear, *Atomic Habits*, 2018.
3. Richard G. Tedeschi and Lawrence G. Calhoun, "The Posttraumatic Growth Inventory: Measuring the Positive Legacy of Trauma," *Journal of Traumatic Stress* 9, no. 3 (1996): 455–71.

15. This Is Not the End

1. American Psychological Association, *The Road to Resilience* (Washington, DC: APA, 2020).
2. Doidge, *The Brain That Changes Itself*, 2007.
3. Attributed to Carl Jung, as cited in modern psychological literature and interpretations; original source unverified.

About the Author

Mairin Moore Cane is an entrepreneur, speaker, and resilience advocate who knows what it means to break down—and build again. For more than two decades, she has led teams, built community, and created meaningful experiences, all while navigating the complexities of chronic illness, motherhood, and personal reinvention.

As co-owner and Chief Strategy Officer, Mairin helped build a national company from the ground up starting in 2000, shaping its culture and strategy through seasons of both growth and challenge. Her people-first leadership centers service, empowers teams, and emphasizes values over shortcuts—an approach she carries into all of her work today.

She also leads the Sisterhood of Success, a personal and professional development company offering masterminds, networking, and leadership workshops to support women in every stage of their journey.

For nearly twenty years, Mairin has curated impactful events—both locally and internationally—creating experiences that bring people together in growth, celebration, and transformation. Today, much of that same work happens at her private event and agrotourism space in the Pacific Northwest, dedicated to sustainability, intentionality, and meaningful connection —built, as she proudly says, from hobby and heart.

Her leadership and voice have brought her to the table with creatives and executives at brands like Nike, Microsoft, Amazon, VRBO, and Keen. She has spoken to rooms across industries, consulted with emerging leaders, and supported those navigating growth on their own terms.

Mairin's writing began with poetry and short stories in her youth, and she later became a co-author in a collaborative work. This book marks her solo debut—and the beginning of a new chapter. Living with chronic illness, she is a fierce advocate for self-trust, gentle strength, and redefining success on one's own terms. Through her story, she creates space for those who feel unseen, reminding them that resilience isn't just about bouncing back; it's about being rooted and rising in who you authentically are.

She lives in the Pacific Northwest with her husband and business partner of twenty-five years, along with two of their four children still at home, while the other two have begun their own journeys. Of all the titles she holds, the ones that mean the most will always be: Wife. Mom. Mimi.

Thank You For Reading My Book!

If this book spoke to you, I'd love to stay connected. You can find me on Instagram at **@MairinMooreCane**, where I share the heart behind my work, my story, and the platforms I lead. Whether you're curious about **Sisterhood of Success**, or just need a reminder that you're not alone —my door is open.

Let's keep growing, together.

If you're ready for more encouragement, resources, and connection, scan the code below.

I can't wait to grow with you.

Scan the QR Code:

*I appreciate your interest in my book and value your feedback,
as it helps me improve future versions. I would appreciate it if you
could leave your invaluable review on Amazon.com with your feedback.
Thank you!*

www.ingramcontent.com/pod-product-compliance
Lightning Source LLC
LaVergne TN
LVHW011327080426
835513LV00006B/229